ROGER WRIGHT

FINDING WORK WHEN THERE ARE NO JOBS

- STOP NETWORKING
- TELL YOUR STORY
- START THINKING DIFFERENTLY

Finding Work When There Are No Jobs
By Roger Wright
Think Different Press

Published by Think Different Press, Chicago, IL

Printed and bound in the USA
Cover design and interior layout | www.pearcreative.ca

Library of Congress Control Number: 2013931055
ISBN: 978-0-9889043-0-9
BUSINESS & ECONOMICS / Careers / Job Hunting

ATTENTION CORPORATIONS, UNIVERSITIES, COLLEGES AND PROFESSIONAL ORGANIZATIONS:

Quantity discounts are available on bulk purchases of this book for educational, gift purposes, or as premiums for increasing magazine subscriptions or renewals. Special books or book excerpts can also be created to fit specific needs. For information, please contact Think Different Press, www.findingwork.org

To my wife Maria, for her heart and soul.

And to my parents, George and Barbara Wright, for all the dreams.

TABLE OF CONTENTS

The way we find work has gone wrong.

The purpose of this book is to set it right. For you.

INTRODUCTION

Why take this journey? Two reasons. The first reason is easy, and obvious.

You need to find work.

But the second reason is much harder to wrap your head around, because it can easily get lost, crushed under the sheer weight of that first reason. The second reason for this journey is that the way talented, honest, well-intentioned people find work has gone brutally wrong.

Just when we needed it the most, the way we find work doesn't work, and the immensity of the need to find work can feel big enough to block out the sun.

When work was readily available, we used shortcuts, the so-called rules of resume writing and job searches that haven't changed in decades, and when jobs became harder and harder to find, those shortcuts, those rules, no longer worked either.

The search for work has become like driving through an endless field of tall grass, with occasional signposts appearing out of the sameness that say something like: "Job Ahead. Just bring a perfect resume." Jammed to the ceiling of your backseat are all the instruction books on how to write that perfect resume. In those books, lots of good advice; almost none of which is really wrong.

The problem is … you've read those books. Chances are, you know how to network, write resumes, and interview.

But it's either been so long since you've looked for work, or you've been looking for work for so *long* that the rules you thought you knew no longer apply. They just aren't leading you to any success.

All you want is a set of instructions. Even though you know that no simple set of instructions will cover it, you still wish you had some kind of guide.

So all too often, you're at that all too familiar place, a place where you send your perfect resume or job application to the man or woman who advertised, and you hope, and keep going, because it's all you know how to do.

But there's no callback, and no job.

If you've ever felt that the search for work is another planet where you don't belong, a planet where you're always thirsty and there's no water—then this book is for you.

The journey we'll take here isn't easy. Especially since you don't know exactly where you'll end up. So you will be frustrated. You'll want to wave your hands above your head and shout, "Can't you just tell me the answer? What's the secret?"

Panic will do that, and there's no panic like the panic of having no work. Instruction books are comfortable. They feel better ... they can often suggest that there is, in fact, some sort of magic answer. "Do these 5 steps and presto! You're employed!"

This book does something different. It offers no generalized answers, no magic. This book sets out to accomplish a much tougher task: to actually change the way you think about finding work. Because only by thinking differently about the search for work are you finally going to start to feel how temporary your stay on that strange planet of joblessness has to be. Only by thinking differently will you finally be able to stand up high enough to see over that tall grass and say, "Hey! Look! There's my path to work. Uniquely, individually *mine*."

Instead of instructions, this book will start a lot of conversations, beginning with that most powerful of questions: "What if?"

There are dozens of stories in this book. None of them are cookbook recipes on how to find work. Think of the stories as "thought-prompters." Their sole purpose is to prompt your thinking on how to create your own, individual path to finding work. Some stories will leave you scratching your head and thinking, "That's nice. But how can I use the point of this story to help me find work?" Some of what you read here will require more thought.

Then there will be the stories that change everything for just you. Stories that trigger what people through the ages have called "an epiphany." A sudden realization about finding work that you have never really thought about, or thought about enough, or acted on. After you read one of the stories in this book, you'll remember it, apply some shred of the story to your own very personal situation, and once again you'll start asking yourself, "What if I...?"

The point? No magic answers. What we will do here is together figure out ways to *think differently* about finding work.

Why Think Differently About Job Search?

Job search has become the most diabolical of systems. It's a system that looks fine on the outside; but from the inside, it is slowly killing souls, costing money and wasting time. Like a devil with a winning smile dressed up in a $2,000 suit with not a pointed horn in sight.

As anyone who's been through it already knows, when a person sits down at the computer and starts tossing resumes out into cyberspace, stands in line and fills out applications, pays people to fashion a resume that must surely be better because it's paid for—most of the time, nothing happens.

Watch the terror-stricken eyes of a person reading job ads as she slowly realizes, "Wait! Nothing here describes me!"

Watch what happens when a recruiter lies about a job because their client just lied to them or could not express what they wanted in the first place.

Job search becomes a barren and cold place where people work really hard and nothing happens. But most of all, it's lonely. The kind of lonely uniquely and sharply felt while standing in a big crowd of people.

We have equated work search with job search. The result is an isolated, demoralizing, illogical path down that rabbit hole where all the unread old resumes go.

Where does the problem start?

Job Search vs. Work Search

We forget that *work* and *jobs* are not always the same. Simple point, right?

Not really. Often the two words are used interchangeably. As if the difference between the two words doesn't matter, and we're saying the same thing two different ways.

But when there are no jobs, it matters.

It goes beyond being a matter of wording because *work* still exists. *Work* will not go away. Jobs, on the other hand, are a different story, and one you already know.

There are a couple of other really good reasons to draw a line in your mind separating work and jobs. First, common sense tells us that finding work gives us a much larger target than finding a job. Second, competing for a job means you're standing in a line with two, two hundred, or maybe two thousand others.

The Job Search Line - A line that *might not lead anywhere.*

But where does one go to stand in The Work Search Line? There isn't one; because finding work demands new and different ways of thinking. We can't all do it the same way … how I found work is going to be different than the way you find work.

Job search is that familiar pattern of filling out the application or sending out the resume and patiently waiting while nothing happens. Job search can also be waiting on the corner for a chance to do day labor and never really knowing if The Man (or Woman) will be by to pick you up. A job search is a rote, step-by-step process.

But work search requires a whole different approach. It requires figuring out the path that's right for you.

Job Search books are all about following steps. Recipes. Take two tablespoons of resume and mix with a networking lunch, dress right at a job interview and your offer letter is in the mail. Except it's not.

There's a Better Way

Throughout history, human beings have turned to storytelling as a way to encourage action, prompt new ways of thinking, innovate, and explore. Call them parables, myths, best practices, or blog posts; in this book we'll just call them stories. But instead of just reading them, we'll use them.

Using a story means taking what you read and translating it into action. How does that work? Imagine holding a piece of clay, knowing that inside is a diamond. That diamond is the element of the story that resonates for you. That diamond prompts another thought—usually one that isn't even in the story—and that thought prompts another and pretty soon you're picking up the phone to call someone who knows someone who can help you find work.

The stories here are overflowing with ideas, with emotion and images, the larger themes that span the daily lives of individuals and currents of thought that could apply anywhere. Stories that get you to think about that all-important "*what if?*" question we mentioned earlier.

At the end of each story, we'll encourage your own personal "what-if" way of thinking with a section called "Connecting to Action." Here, we'll offer questions and observations on the stories that will help you bring them back down to earth, to your own search.

As we keep saying, there is no magic here. No experts. No one-size-fits-all, "*write the perfect resume and your problems are over*" theory. Stories lift all the strictures of those old outdated rules and allow you to think about finding work in far more imaginative and productive ways. That doesn't mean every story will prompt new thoughts. Some won't. Then there will be other stories you read here will that open a door you hadn't even realized was there.

So what we'll do here is use a very old method to help you think in ways that will get you somewhere new.

THE FIVE

The journey begins with five principles. Think of these as lumps of clay, ready to be molded by your hands alone. It's these principles that form your new way of thinking. From them, you'll start seeing your search differently.

The five principles are always in play. They form the framework for how you structure your search.

As you work with each of the five principles around which our journey is organized, a new way of thinking will result. You'll begin to see that *"can't you just give me the answer?"* is not the right question. It's not even a useful question. Because the real question, the one that makes this journey different, is this: "How do I think differently about finding work? Not like the experts or advisors or people I know who have been successful. Not people who have followed rules."

How do *I* find work?

FIRST: Tell Your Story

Not: write a good resume. Tell *YOUR* Story. Any piece of it, anywhere, to anyone. Here's why: we've reduced our stories to resumes. In doing so, we've left out what's most important. Trying to stack up against all the other resumes, we've left out who we *are*.

By not telling our own story, we miss conveying what makes us the most capable, the person who can say *"this is why I can fill the need you have."*

SECOND: Add Music

This one sounds the strangest and is the hardest to understand. This is, of course, a clue that it might be the most powerful. But as you sit there wondering what this means, try a quick experiment.

See how long it takes you to remember the jingle of a TV commercial. Got it?

Okay. Then here's the point. See how easy that was? The music captured the product someone was selling, differentiated it from all the others, and placed it off in its own little corner of your brain.

What if you were able to do the exact same thing in your work search: differentiate yourself from everyone else who wanted to work? What better tools to use than the elements of music? You don't have to sing. You don't have to play an instrument. Just consider for a moment: what if the elements of music—rhythm, harmony, and so on—prompted new ways of thinking about how to differentiate you from the rest of the world?

The rhythm of being able to perform a task consistently.

The harmony of working with a team.

The beat of building a place for yourself in the working world.

THIRD: Communitize

We'll say good-bye to what used to be called *networking* right now.

Simply by turning "community" into an action verb, you aren't just going to a network lunch and standing in the corner talking to competitors about how no one has jobs. You aren't following a script of conversation starters. You don't join every single online networking site, only to get bombarded by e-mails that don't apply to your search at all.

When you communitize, you become woven into the fabric of a community—any community. Because communities have needs and needs are springboards to work.

The action in communitizing comes from being able to provide an answer to the question: if I were part of this community, what need could I fill?

When you communitize, you look for the needs of a community from the *inside*. Not from the outside like a networker. In the needs of a community as seen from an insider's perspective, you find clues to finding work. The Communitizing Principle stands on the shoulders of the groundbreaking work of Bob Beaudine's book, "The Power of Who." Beaudine writes, "if you really want to make a significant change in your life, don't go external in your approach, go internal." Communitizing is the action of "going internal," finding work from the inside of a community.

FOURTH: Solve a Mystery

Perhaps best shown by my friend Bill, whose phone number is on my speed dial because every time something even thinks about breaking in my house, he's the guy I call.

He comes over and fixes it. But that's not the part applicable to finding work. It's the part where he makes it look easy that's important. To me what he does is a mystery, one that only he can solve.

For example, smoke comes from behind a wall. I panic. He unscrews two screws, replaces something metal, and he's done. Maybe thirty seconds of work, but work that was a mystery to me.

Now, what would it do for your work search if you could solve mysteries? I mean any kind of mystery. As every single frontline worker and every soldier knows, sometimes what happens on the front line really is a mystery to a boss or a General. Ever watch a senior executive try to work a copy machine or send a fax? Anything can be a mystery. The question to explore is: how do you make all the mysteries you can solve become a part of your story? Because solving mysteries, once again, means that you are filling needs.

FIFTH: Practice Stewardship

Job search manuals are chock-full of words like *duties*, *responsibilities*, and *tasks*. That's a stark contrast to our final principle, practicing stewardship. Or put another way, taking care of something bigger than you. It could be a building, a truck, a store, a shelf, a town, or the world's literature.

Where's the *action* here? It's in answering the question, "What if I could figure out new ways of taking care of something bigger than myself?" Even better, "What if I was already practicing stewardship in one place?

Could there be a chance that I could do it somewhere else? Perhaps a place where I'd find work?"

If this book were a meal, the Five Principles would be the spoon, fork, knife, cup, and plate. The stories that illustrate each principle would be dinner. Each "Connecting to Action" section would be dessert.

But as we set the table and prepare to eat, another question comes to mind.

How did we get so hungry?

PART ONE:
WHERE DID WE GO WRONG?

How did we get in this job search line in the first place?

Now, that is not a pretty story. If you're already there, you already know it. You just might want to skip the next section of the book, because it's depressing. Or at least wait until you're having a good day. That's one of the things about standing in the job search line; you go from very, very bad days to good days and back again. A rollercoaster you didn't want to ride.

So by all means, feel free to skip ahead to Part Two and begin to use the stories there to think differently about finding work.

But if you're standing in the job search line and you feel like you're totally alone … read Part One. Because as all of us who have stood in that line know, despite all the people in line with you, it can be a very lonely place.

If you've never stood in the job search line, perhaps you know someone who has, and you might want to take a quick peek for their sake.

Because standing in that line is worse that you could ever imagine.

Ready to go?

Remember, we warned you. This part's ugly.

The Job Search Line

There is nothing fun about this line.

It's the giant, universal line to find a job. As you stand in the line, it barely moves. Up at the front, you've heard tell there's a job. But you can't see the front of the line.

No one is smiling in this line. Sound familiar?

In the job search line, almost everything you know about finding work has been turned upside down.

- EXPERIENCE: can hurt you

- WELL-WRITTEN RESUMES: mean nothing

- PERFORMANCE or RESULTS: don't matter

- LOYALTY or LONGEVITY: is a quaint memory

- WELL-RUN COMPANIES: are no longer the goal

- HAVING A CONVERSATION: is rare

- ANONYMITY: must be maintained

- A JOB ADVERTISED: often doesn't mean it exists

Perhaps the most diabolical characteristic of the job search line is that if you don't look hard, everything can seem just fine. Business as usual.

There are lots of reasons for that. All of which have to do with job search being a system. A whirring, humming machine that clicks along as you become a part of it.

You assume that all is well. You'll just send out a few more resumes. If something is wrong here it must be your fault. Right?

So you turn back to the Internet job search site, type in the name of a job, and start pushing resumes out into cyberspace. You're working. So you must get something back from your work, right? Hmmm. No response? Better work harder.

That goes on until a stray thought floats across your mind. "Wait a minute, Mr. Advertising Employer. Tell me again why I'm not allowed to know your name?"

The Job Search Line can—above all—be deceptive and time-killing when you don't have time to waste.

So to make sure you get out of that line and on to the business of finding work, let's take a very hard look at the Job Search Line.

It Starts with Labeling

When you get in the Job Search Line, you get labeled.

Labeling people always leaves someone out. Labels like *unemployed* or *underemployed* are no less exclusionary, because standing under those convenient labels are individual human beings. Every single person's story is unique.

Perhaps you wouldn't give yourself a label. For you, there's more to it than that. You used to have a paycheck. Now you don't. Or the paycheck you now have has a much lower number on it.

Maybe you're a person who used to look for work but now you don't even try anymore. Why should you? Nothing happens when you do.

Maybe your job search is more like a story where nothing happened.

See? You just got in line and already there's a problem. A label. One that really doesn't capture who you are and what you have to offer.

Are You Moving Yet?

Now labeled, you stand in a really long line. Shuffling slowly toward the possible job at the front. The line stretches around 3 city blocks, winds its way out of town, travels past empty houses, deserted farms, and barren fields, and stretches on out to the next town, where it passes abandoned factories, boarded-up storefronts, and crumbling parking lots in front of empty office buildings. You can't see much of anything beyond the person in front of you because it's dark as night.

No one speaks. Above all, it's quiet. A disturbing quiet.

When you first took your place in the line, somebody handed you a book. In the book were the basics of how to get a job. Most everyone still has the book, though some lay scattered along the ribbon of people winding their way across a dark, still wasteland where jobs once grew.

What's in the book? Cautionary tales of chewing gum in job interviews, warnings about letting the new boss know you were fired for punching the old boss in the nose, examples of the perfect resume.

All the usual advice. All based on the usual premise that the shortest distance between two points, the shortest distance to the job, is a straight line. It's a logical assumption. So you stand in the line for the job. You might be munching on potato chips watching a daytime talk show or staring blankly at an Internet job board or filling out a profile in an HR office. But you are in some form of this line.

The line inches forward so slowly you can feel wrinkles in your face growing deeper.

Finally, you get to the front of the line. You are dressed in your finest job interview clothes. Your hair is perfect. Your handshake is firm. You attempt to look the hiring manager straight in the eye, but he or she won't make eye contact, and a thought flashes into your brain like a buzz saw.

There is no job. It's already gone, if it was ever here at all.

Now what?

You stand there dumbfounded. Not sure where or how to move. You've gone through the line. You've worked as hard as you know how to work. You've made job search a full-time job. Done everything asked of you. Nothing happened.

The way the system is set up didn't work for you.

So you begin to wonder. What if?

- What if you had your own line? Why not? The one you were standing in with everyone else didn't work.

- What if the entire *system* surrounding how we search for jobs does more harm than good? Ever spend a moment on an Internet job board? Apply for a job that doesn't exist? Useful, fairly paid *work* and not a *job* would be a better goal for you.

- What if the best path for you, in *your* search for work, was not a straight line? As silly as it might sound, what if the path to work for you required some zigging and zagging?

- What if there was a way to *think differently about finding work*?

PART TWO:
TELLING YOUR STORY

The Five. They prompt a way to think differently about finding work. The first of the five is: Tell Your Story.

Any piece of it. Anywhere. To anyone. As I pointed out at the beginning of this book, we've reduced our stories to resumes. In doing so, we've left out what's most important.

This is not saying that a concise summary of your past is not important. But the quest for the perfect resume has become far too large a part of the accepted thinking about finding work.

Describing the perfect resume is easy. The perfect resume or job application is the one that helps you have a conversation with someone about work that they need done.

The real problem is that the magical quest for the perfect resume has carried us away from the importance of being able to tell your story in other forms. Whether it's in writing or in conversation.

Telling your story starts with listening. What you're listening for are any types of connections you might have to the person you're talking with. Maybe the connection is something you have in common. Or maybe the connection is simply something you hear that sparks your interest. It could be anything. People, places, likes, dislikes, wishes, dreams, ideas. You are listening for a connection that will allow you to form a bond with that person; one that will differentiate you in their mind.

That person can be anyone. Remember that your road to work is not a straight line. It zigs and zags from person to person. You simply never know who can be a connection on your road to finding work.

As you listen, you can begin to raise your own potential connections to that person. Bits and pieces of who you are. Bits and pieces that naturally connect to what you've heard from the other person. Those natural, human connections are what you're looking for. Like, "You went to a big public high school? So did I! I remember when ..."

Suddenly you're telling a story.

Into that story you toss an example of how you used some sort of talent. Not work history. Talent. For example, you went into a totally disorganized situation and found the right tools and the right methodology and the right people to help you get it back on track. Talent is a picture of what makes you unique. Specifically, traits, skills, knowledge, and instinct in action, all of which come naturally to you. The stuff no one really taught you. The stuff you somehow always knew.

When you've mastered the first principle of telling your story, you'll know it. Here's what will happen: you will have a command of your story that is so strong that you can grab the right piece of the story right out of the air at just the right time with just the right person.

Sound hard? It is. But it's also how you begin to build what it takes to find work when there are no jobs. When you really start thinking about it, you've already done this. Think back to a moment when you have really impressed someone. You've been having a conversation, they make a point, you answer with a story that shows you know exactly what the other person is talking about, and they say "Yeah! You get what I'm saying!"

That moment is our first principle—tell your story—in action.

So in this chapter we'll look at that principle in action from a variety of angles. Not in job interviews, because remember, the path to a job starts long before the job interview. We'll look at what happens when there is no story, we'll look at telling a story where you made a difference, how we all sometimes fool ourselves when we tell a story, the kinds of impressions we leave when we tell a story, the role of honesty, and telling stories that include assuming responsibility when things go wrong, just as you accept accolades when things go right.

Take a moment or two with each story. Let them do their work. The work of turning thoughts into action. Ask yourself, "*How can I use the ways I tell my story to help me connect to work?*"

Where do you start? Imagine your story is money. A rich, vibrant story connecting with people, purpose, and with the world means lots of money. No story means no money.

So the question becomes, "How do you make your story worth more?"

WORK SEARCH CURRENCY

What's your story worth? The big story that includes everything there is to know about you. The story no one really knows but you. All the billions of moments that no one really saw but you. Can you instantaneously tell any single part of that story?

Most of us divide up our story and put each part into a different box. In this dull gray box I'll toss my skills. Over here in this green box I'll put my talents. In the blue box with the big lock I'll put the personal stuff, and in the orange box I'll place all the really immediate and important stuff that makes me someone worth hiring. That hard-to-describe stuff, like "*I care about the job I do.*"

Rather than compartmentalizing, what if you were to build a larger, richer story made up of all the stuff that was really important? What if you started thinking of your story as the currency you used to find work?

The more quality bits and pieces of story you have and can tell, the better equipped you are for the work search.

Reducing your story to a resume is like having a wallet filled only with one-dollar bills. Expanding your story would be like stuffing the wallet with fistfuls of cash.

Let's use this first story to see what happens when a person has no story. An empty wallet. As you read this story, ask yourself,

"*How can I make the currency of my story more valuable?*"

First, consider:

- What happens when a person doesn't have a story?

- How does your story figure in your search for work?

- How does a resume or job application differ from a story?

- Are there parts of your story that you are leaving out?

THE STORY: Drawing a Blank

This morning the wind chill in Chicago hit zero. Just before the sun rose over the frozen lake I heard, "Roger, you'd better come downstairs. You've got to see this."

Maria was standing at the kitchen window, looking out at the back yard.

I figured it would be a bird. Two giant pine trees frame our garage. Like bustling and chattering bird condos. Birds of all colors, both tropical rainbow travelers and tiny brown chickadees and sparrows who blend right in and become part of the rhythm of the city. Chirping visitors who stop to visit us here in Chicago on their way to warm and distant lands.

Once a flock of brilliant yellow canaries even found their way to our tiny patch of city yard.

So I figured she'd show me a dead bird.

The gray November winds were howling as if they knew no answers. This year, flocks of birds, which use the big lake to migrate south for the winter, have been blown off course even more than usual. Blown into all these big houses and shiny buildings, none of which were here when the birds first began this journey centuries ago. Smacking into the buildings at an alarming rate.

Dead birds on the lawns, the sidewalks, and in the streets.

Then there is a slowdown in city services that clean the streets, because the city, like everyone else, is running out of money. So the litter of dead birds is common.

"Is it a bird?" I asked.

"No."

"Is it a possum or raccoon?" I yelled.

"No."

"Not a coyote or deer?"

"It's something we've never seen before," she answered, motioning me over to our back kitchen window. She pointed outside to the ground in the very center of our little city lawn. There on the brutally cold, November grass were the remnants of a human's makeshift bed.

A stained pillow pulled from a Dumpster. Scraggly thin blanket that couldn't have kept our nameless traveler warm, and some assorted rags used to cover up against that wind that kept blowing the birds into the high-rises and houses.

While we were warm inside our little house last night, somebody had spent the night on our back lawn.

The pillow still showing the indentation of where this wandering soul of dark alleys had finally laid their weary head down for the night. The back gate swinging open to the alley; perhaps our visitor had left as dawn broke.

Putting on my work gloves and grabbing a large plastic garbage bag to collect the remnants of the makeshift bed and deposit them in our trash can, I couldn't help but wonder where our visitor was right then. Or where he would be later that day when I was worrying about things like picking up a suit at the dry cleaners.

I wondered if he was hungry.

Did he have a job? Did he have shoes?

In the pile of clothes I found one boot.

I tossed the bag of his bedclothes, including that one boot, into my trash can.

I wondered if his other foot was warm.

WORK HISTORY THAT MAKES A DIFFERENCE

Do You Communicate What Matters?

When you tell somebody else your work history, do you leave out examples of doing something that made a difference?

Not only in a job interview. Anywhere. Even in the briefest of conversations. By omitting the really important parts of your story, could you be, in effect, leaving money on the table?

The forms you often need to fill out in a *job* search certainly encourage you to ignore what's most important. Even when you have to fill out the same information twice. The dates of employment, reasons for leaving—all those usual stock pieces of information history. You've got that covered. But what about the importance of the people you worked with? What it meant to be part of a team? The satisfaction of getting something done? That feeling of being tired that comes after doing good work? Doing work that mattered. Something that made a difference. No matter what it was.

Use this story to take you back in time through your own work history. Try to avoid comparing yourself to someone else, to those who cure cancers, lead nations, or make movies. It's not about making a difference compared with someone else. The question is simply, "Did I make a difference?"

As you read this story, consider:

- When you tell the story of your work history, are you including examples of where you made a difference?

- If the dates, locations, and details of past jobs were somehow erased from your mind, what would you remember?

THE STORY: Making a Real Difference

My first job out of school was as a counselor on the adolescent psychiatric ward of a major Chicago hospital. We took care of the kids during the 23 hours a day when they weren't seeing their psychiatrists.

Located on the 23rd floor of a tower overlooking Lake Michigan, the building looked like somebody had rolled a circular cone of concrete into a tube and punched tiny spaceship portholes for windows. A circle of concrete that could blast off into space any second. Sometimes, when a kid would lose it, I could imagine the building launching into outer space.

Working nights, the last task of the shift would be to make breakfast for the kids. Celeste was one of those kids.

With huge sad brown eyes, she was always quietly polite. She'd spend about 45 minutes rearranging the dry Rice Krispies with her spoon and agreeing to drink the orange juice I served her, sometimes even laughing when I pretended to be "Maurice" the pretentious French waiter, yelling in mock indignation that she just better like this meal!

On brutally cold winter mornings, when the clock at the corner bank read 6 degrees and the wind chill was 10 below zero, the rising of the sun over Lake Michigan would shoot beams of light through the porthole windows of the locked ward. Light beams illuminating Celeste numbly doing battle with the task of trying to eat her breakfast. Perhaps pain and hunger were driving her wild. But from the outside, she just looked numb.

Celeste's father was a college professor. Radiating intelligence just by the way he moved. The same big brown eyes. I remember he'd be as quiet as his daughter was when he came to visit.

Ellen was the other girl with an eating disorder. Shorter and even slimmer than Celeste, with narrow eyes. She almost never spoke at all. It seemed like what she really wanted was to make herself invisible. Her father was a military man, a big man who wore his winter coat like a cape around his shoulders. When he'd visit, he'd bark out questions as if they were commands to all of us "mental health workers."

Every time he was buzzed into the ward, it took only about 15 seconds for all of us to know that the General had arrived.

Some of the kids you connect with, some you don't. Ellen would ask for grapes for breakfast. She'd push them around her plate just like Celeste did with the Rice Krispies. When I'd look away for a moment, one would be gone. But she never laughed at my bad French waiter imitations. Never laughed much at anything.

The first time I ever made Celeste laugh was on an evening field trip to a giant mall called Water Tower Place. A glittering bauble of retail white lights and marble and glass where beads of water jump from fountains, hypnotically splashing down and diverting the attention of both kids and grown-ups away from the fact that nobody really needs anything that's sold in the place.

It was also a luxury condo residence where Oprah owned a place on one of the upper floors of the adjoining Ritz-Carlton hotel. I was assigned to Celeste that night. Our job was to take the kids wherever they wanted to go in the mall. So I turned our little outing into a journey to find Oprah.

Making fun of every store we entered. Approaching strangers to politely ask if they'd seen Oprah in the vicinity. Explaining that sometimes she hid in plain sight by wearing a giant teased blond wig and sunglasses.

By the end of the outing, Celeste had probably spent at least three-quarters of the time laughing. She even began to make fun of me for liking the cool grown-up toys in the Sharper Image store.

That was before I cajoled her to sit in one of their thousand-dollar massage lounge chairs and put on headphones that played sounds of bubbling streams, while I mouthed, "Is this cool or what?"

This was my first week on the job. I liked hanging out with that kid more than I liked anything else.

I really didn't think too much about it, other than it being fun. Until the next day at the staff meeting. That's when I found out that no one, not the doctors, the nurses, or the other counselors, had ever seen Celeste laugh like that.

So, much to my great shock, I was asked right then and there at that staff meeting to stand up and explain my technique.

I remember my answer from over 30 years ago as if it was an hour ago. I stood up, cleared my throat, and said, "Geez, I don't know. I guess we just hung out."

Nobody knew how to respond to that tiny piece of profundity, so the staff meeting just went on.

Soon after that, Celeste was discharged. She didn't look much different than the day she came in. But who was I to judge? She was gone. I never expected to run into her again.

Three years later I was working at a bookstore. Standing in the window behind the counter, ringing up sales of books. It was a lazy, sidewalk strolling city summer evening. I happened to turn around from the register and look out through the window on to the sidewalk.

She was looking at a book in the window. Those same big brown eyes now pools of shimmering self-confidence. As if that skinny scared little girl now existed only in a memory. A memory to keep her strong. She looked up from that book and met my eyes directly, recognition like blazing fireworks sparkling across the summer sky.

She said nothing, just took one step back, inviting me to look at her and share the wonder and then echo her unspoken thought: "Just look at what happened to me! Isn't this amazing? I'm okay now."

A smile, dazzling.

She lifted her hand, gave me a quick short wave, and then pointed at me. As if to say, "Look! You made a difference!"

HOW DO OTHERS SEE ME?

Does Your Authenticity Come Through?

When are you really being you? Do you act differently when no one is watching?

That's a pretty tough question to answer honestly. How would you know?

But what if you could know? Think of the confidence you'd have if you knew whether your authentic, real self was coming through to others. Then think about how you could use that confident self-awareness to tell your story.

In this story, Barack Obama, before he took office as President, is "offstage." No cameras or speeches to make. The narrator is standing on the other side of a soccer field.

As you join the kids' soccer game being watched by both the President-elect and the narrator, ask yourself, "What impression do I leave from afar?" Or even more important, "What kind of an impression do I leave when I am most authentically being me?" Consider:

- If someone watched me from a distance, how would they describe me?

- Is that description one I'd want?

- How could becoming more self-aware help my work search?

THE STORY: When the Cameras Stop Rolling

Malia Obama probably wasn't sure if her Dad would make it home from work to watch her soccer game this past Friday night.

He's been pretty busy lately.

But her Mom and her little sister would be there.

The flow of the kids moving the ball down the soccer field, under the lights of a chilly autumn night. The families chatting on the sidelines. The starlight glow of downtown Chicago rising up from the north. Malia at midfield shouts "Mom!" The woman with grace and presence whose eyes never once leave her daughter, no matter who else she speaks to, waves back and sends a radiant smile.

In that one wave and smile, you see hope come alive before your very eyes.

Then just a few minutes after eight, something like a shift in the earth's gravity occurs. To the casual observer, nothing in this scene has changed. That pull of the earth's power must have been imagined.

The true city dweller will feel it first, before they even see it. Blink your eyes and the men appear.

Ringing the shadows of the soccer field are people with guns. Serious people with guns. Like oak trees that move. The phrase *"not on my watch"* flashes through your head.

They aren't moving. But when you blink your eyes, somehow their positions have changed. Something about the way they appear calms your breathing. You never really see a gun.

Instinctively you know. These are the good guys.

With that feeling of true safety, you remember the real secret at the heart of the city: we of the city are just a million small towns all strung together. So the kids laugh and kick the soccer ball. As they would anywhere.

Then some skinny guy in a blue baseball cap walks out of the gym next door.

Hands in his pocket, face down, by himself. He walks over to Malia's mom, who has three conversations going simultaneously with folks on the sidelines.

The quiet guy in the blue cap puts his arm around Malia's mom. Shakes hands with a couple of people. Talks with Malia's mom for a minute or two.

The quiet guy in the blue cap to whom nobody in the crowd really paid all that much attention squats down so he is face-to-face with Malia's little sister Sasha. She lifts the brim of his cap.

Standing in the shadows behind Sasha, you see what she's seeing up close. You see that smile. That smile shining with the very power and the glory of the city lights behind it. That smile almost ready to take its place in American history.

You can't hear what he's saying to his youngest daughter. But from this distance you do hear her giggle.

The father takes the daughter's hand. The younger daughter. The one who is not in the game. The one who was destined to not get a lot of attention tonight.

They move back deeper into the shadows, behind the sideline crowd. Still watched by that quiet show of force here to keep them absolutely safe.

Father and daughter have a foot race.

While the soccer game is still going on. Just the two of them. Sasha and her Dad take off together, both running at full speed, fast and then faster. Sasha laughing and laughing at the finish line, where her father swoops down and picks her up.

The smile again, for his daughter at that moment. It was just for her.

His youngest daughter's giggle, somehow like music of a promise that connects us all.

This past Friday night in Chicago, Malia Obama's team won the game.

CONNECTING TO ACTION

- In the story, there is no dialogue. Yet there are at least half a dozen messages communicated by President Barack Obama. If someone were to watch you from afar, what would you want your messages to be?

- How will you make sure your messages are in your story?

Try this experiment. Pick someone who will give you an honest opinion. Ask how you would come across in the first 10 seconds of a conversation about searching for work. Ask that person three questions.

- Would your authenticity come through in those 10 seconds?

- Would you come across as authentic no matter who was watching you?

- What is it you have to do to make sure that your authenticity comes through when you are telling your story?

IS HONESTY OVERRATED?

It's one thing to sound and appear authentic, to really be yourself, in the way you deliver your story; it can mean something else to be honest.

Being honest sounds so simple. But it can also come off as self-righteous. A cliché. Honesty can be a lot tougher in the work search than one might assume. Does honesty mean telling everybody everything?

As you read the story of one man who built a career on honesty, you'll see that honesty also comes coupled with so many other factors. The man was also paid to entertain, which he does quite brilliantly. The man works in a very competitive field. Like all of us, he is so much more than the sum of a single abstract notion. But there is so much more to his story than the honesty. Consider as you read this story:

- What does honesty mean to you?

- How does your definition compare to others'?

- Can honesty harm you in the work search? How?

THE STORY: An Honest Guy at the Coffee Shop

Before Howard Stern and a thousand bad shock-jock imitators, there was the man right now sitting farthest from the fireplace at a small table in a Caribou Coffee shop on Ashland Avenue, wrapped in a steel-gray bitter cold winter Monday afternoon in Chicago.

He was speaking in low tones to the nondescript woman across the table in what was obviously a business meeting; he once spoke to half a million people a day.

Born from a bad-boy image and known for both big and small publicity bits through the almost thirty years he carved out a career at the top of the radio game, he influenced anyone and everyone who ever sat down in front of a radio microphone, looked up to see the "ON THE AIR" light flash, and then tried to entertain.

This guy was honest.

Brutal, sometimes obnoxious, always entertaining; whether you loved or hated him, he was honest. Honest like you wouldn't believe honest.

At the heart of that honesty was his habit of literally sharing his life with those of us who listened through the years. Those of us who, you might say, grew up with him. I remember the microphone in the delivery room as his first son, now married with his own family, was born. I remember hearing his son's first cry, his dad's wondrous sighs of delight, and his wife's resounding joy as she said to her firstborn, "Don't worry. We'll take care of you."

I remember the sudden death of a member of his radio gang. Gone way too young.

I remember speaking with this big gray-haired gentleman in the corner of the Caribou personally and on the phone in my role as a management consultant, working through some ideas on how to reorganize his production company. A plan that was eventually shelved when he broke down and hired a professional producer.

He's no longer on the air. The market changed. No one pays anyone a million dollars a year to talk on "free" radio anymore.

But he's still here. Still out there pitching. Right over there in the corner of this Caribou on a Monday afternoon. Guy kept a lot of people safe on the roads by making sure they paid attention. He generated oceans of laughter. The on-air fights he'd have with his wife, herself a force of intelligent nature and grace, probably saved more than a few marriages by showing those of us who listened how to really fight and then love again.

Not having him on the radio shifts the cosmic balance of the city. The echoes of an absent voice blow icily down the snow-slicked streets. But as I walk by his table toward the door, I think, he's not done yet. He will not go quietly. This won't be the year he takes his leave.

To honor his honesty, I quietly leave him to his meeting without saying a word and, with my coffee in hand, walk out the door thinking "Thank you Steve Dahl."

WHO OR WHAT TO BLAME

Does blame play a role in your work search story? Are you blaming yourself? The economy? Past employers? Blame is *always* somewhere on the work search path. Because somewhere, something went wrong.

This story includes an element of blame. As you read it, think about the role blame plays in telling your story. Consider:

- Do you, perhaps even unknowingly, communicate even a trace of blame when you get to the part in your story where you have to explain why you are looking for work?

- What would change if blame was eliminated from your story?

THE STORY: That Time I Cheated

There must have been at least ten of us spread across three floors of the house in the old Wisconsin town. We were college students. We had thoughts like, "Kierkegaard didn't pay utility bills. Why should we?"

We believed eating cheap noodles and tuna fish by candlelight around the scratched round table somebody found in an alley had a certain charm. As did washing our dinner dishes in the dark. Crusty food or water spots on the dishes didn't bother us at all.

Jill and I lived in a tiny room in the basement. We had our own bathroom that included a creaky old shower stall. Dirty gold shag carpeting and wood-paneled walls styled like a northern Wisconsin supper club where neon beer signs sporting smiling grizzly bears hang behind the bar.

Mindy's room was on the first floor right off the dining room. At the center of the house. There was a step up into her room where it was really easy to bang your toe because, like I said, it was usually dark in that house. But there was always really loud music playing so no one could hear the sounds of stubbed toe pain. Or any other sounds that might come out of that room in the middle of the night.

Mindy's mattress, covered with a giant red goose-down cover, was on the floor. So it provided a convenient place to land when clutching a painful aching toe.

Mindy was a gymnast. Specialized in the uneven bars.

If you were to walk past Mindy's room to the front of the house there were two other bedrooms, where the twins Moe and Curly lived. Their names were really Ronald and Dexter. They weren't really twins. We just called them The Twins.

They were the ones who were supposed to pay the bills, which is why the lights were sometimes off. They were also the alpha dogs of the house. Not because they were bigger, richer, or smarter than anybody else. They ruled the roost because for some reason or another, they always seemed to know every single secret, every piece of private business, of everyone in the house.

They knew more about each of us than we knew about ourselves. If somebody had told me they had all our medical records I wouldn't have batted an eye.

I didn't know any secrets. I went to classes and thought about writing and baseball and being in love with Jill. I didn't think about secrets.

At least up until that morning when both Moe and Curly, each sporting an evil grin, and following up the grin with a wink, began calling me "Da Man."

It started the morning after the 3:00 a.m. crash when I tripped on a backpack somebody had left on the dining room floor, yelled "Shit!" and stumbled into Mindy's room and a smiling, warm, Mindy.

I stayed until just before the 6:00 a.m. alarm clock would wake Jill, sleeping like a lamb alone in our room downstairs.

I had been making that dark journey upstairs to Mindy's room every so often for the past few months. Tiptoeing upstairs from the cozy little room in the basement after Jill fell asleep. But it was the first time I had fallen and stubbed my toe.

The next morning as we passed in the dining room, Moe, big grin and wild punch-bowl hair, high-fived me, whispering, "Wooo! You are Da *Man*!" and then motioned at Mindy's door with his chin. "I heard a little ... ah ... stumble last night. Now don't be cute with me and tell me you don't know what I'm saying. How long has this been going on?"

"'Bout a month," I said looking at the floor. Ashamed.

"Hey, dude. You are the man! That chick is totally hot! You don't know how many times I wished I could change myself into the uneven bars and let her practice on me. She must be like ..."

"You're not going to tell Jill, are you?"

"Hey man, it's our secret. Don't worry about it."

"I mean, I don't want to hurt Jill or anything. But Mindy is just so, well..."

Just then Curly strolled in. Put his hand up to high-five me as he passed.

"*You* are Da Man!"

I was terrified Jill would find out and dump me. I loved Jill. I thought about telling her first, before someone else did. But somehow that seemed even more cowardly. I wasn't sure why.

As it turned out, Jill solved the problem for me. She never did find out about Mindy. She did however find out about Sharon. A ceramics major who lived next door.

Jill ended up dumping me for Sharon.

That was our last semester in the house on Park Street. Five of us moved down to Chicago to live on Clifton Street behind a Mexican restaurant. A new start in summer winds after the dark cold floors of that old house. Jill went back to North Carolina for a while and then off to have a life in Northern California.

Across the years of a life speckled with the occasional certainty of black and white interspersed with many tones of gray, I think back to that dark house and wonder what would have happened if Jill had found out about Mindy.

Who would I blame?

Myself? Jill? What would I have done? Tell her a story about needs not met? Take comfort in Moe and Curly singing their Greek chorus chants of approval about what a clever stud I was?

Would I have looked for someone to blame?

Did I deceive? You bet. Did I chip away at the precious diamond of trust? Totally.

Perhaps I could blame the nature of that big dark house because it encouraged me to cheat. My upbringing. My parents. The President of the college for letting us live off campus. Not a lot of supervision in that house.

But what if blame was not the point?

That semester a new book had just come out: Peter Senge's *The Fifth Discipline*. I remember Senge's explanation of how "blame" misses the point when we start thinking of yourselves as all being part of the same connected system. Senge taught that blame would not help. What helps is strengthening your relationship with the other person. Even when that person is an enemy.

Strengthening my relationship with my enemy? That sounds hard.

Blaming is easier. Even now.

CONNECTING TO ACTION

- Reflecting back on the story, who is to blame for the deception in the house?

- In the house, everyone was, like Senge taught, part of the same system. How does being part of the same system as all those seeking work limit your work search?

- How does being part of the same system help your work search?

- Is blame part of your work search story now? How?

- What could change if blaming was no longer part of your work search?

PART THREE:
ADDING MUSIC

Principle #1, "Telling Your Story," was the starting point. Your story will always play a part in your search.

Principle #2, "Adding Music," goes one step further and speaks to the questions: How do I keep making my story more and more powerful? How do I ensure that people will want to listen?

Why do we turn to music here? It's because music can communicate in ways that go far beyond words. Ever listen to a happy person whistle? Or associate a song with a person, place, or thing? Music has always been used to help tell a story.

Why not use it to help tell yours?

Now, showing up at a job interview with a brass band would more likely generate an escort out of the building than it would a job offer. Instead, start thinking about the elements of music as conveyances to tell your story with richness and a substance that simply wasn't there back when all you did was recite the facts of your work history.

Where does adding music start? Instead of only reciting work experience facts, you also include elements that can be equated to elements of music in the way you tell your story. You begin thinking and expressing the value you bring to work in terms of the *rhythm* of being able to perform a task consistently. The *harmony* of working with a team. The *tone* you struck in solving a problem. The *chorus* of agreement you brought to a project. The list goes on. It can be as long as you'd like. By connecting your story to the elements that make up music, you are turning your story into something people will want to listen to.

Adding music is an awfully vague concept—maybe even a bit of a silly one. How do you make it work for you? What do you do next?

Start reading the stories in this section. As you read, ask yourself one question: "If I were to add the element of music that I found in each of these stories to my own work search story, what would change in the way I go about finding work?"

Ask the question. Then listen hard. Perhaps you'll be surprised when a piece of music leads you to an answer.

CAN MUSIC TRANSFORM?

The woman and the piece of music in this story seem to have no connection at all. Yet the music gives her comfort. It soothes her in a very foreign land. It prompts memories. Most startlingly of all, the music prompts her to start working! All of this action paints a picture of a transformation.

The song used here is not well known. But that isn't the point. The point is that the music helped usher in a transformation.

Perhaps a piece of music has done something similar for you. Your song, your music, has energized you. Inspired you. Given you that boost that makes you stand out. Reminded you of what it is that makes you unique. Put another way: it helped you differentiate yourself.

The moment you differentiate yourself is perhaps the single most important moment in the work search. (Except of course for that moment someone says, "You're hired!") Because the moment you differentiate yourself is the moment you take that first giant step out of the job search line. Once you're out of the line, you can really start thinking about and acting on finding work when there are no jobs.

Your music is anything you want it to be. Maybe your music is in the song of a bird, the rumbling of a train rolling down the tracks, the lines in a painting, a dance, or a blasting wall of rock and roll. All that matters is that it's yours.

Great athletes speak of digging deep and finding something extra within themselves to win the game, beat the time, or finish first in the race. Reaching down to that place where mystery blends with talent. Music can be a conduit for that journey.

The science behind music's power is well documented in Daniel Levitan's brilliant *This Is Your Brain on Music: The Science of a Human Obsession*. Religion and music have always been intertwined. If you doubt the connection between music and business, try remembering the last time you heard a commercial without music.

People have been "whistling while they work" forever. In this section we'll do the same. This time, whistling while we work to find you work.

THE STORY: Why Is My Song Different?

Years from now, the sad-eyed young woman in an orange dress, wrapped up against the Chicago cold in a blue goose-down coat, will step outside the Haitian Community Center and walk toward the water.

Every year the quiet ceremony remembering Earthquake Day—January 12, 2010—seems to grow larger. Fifteen thousand Haitians called Chicago home in 2010; a few years later, thousands more did so.

In the Rogers Park neighborhood where she lives a few blocks from the center, the huddled frozen souls of the day are just beginning to fill the streets, the rising winter sun laughing at warmth. The woman offers up a tiny smile, wondering if the tropical sun of the first fourteen years of her life had warmed her bones enough to make it through all the rest of her coming winters.

She remembers fragments of that day in 2010 and its terrible aftermath. The sweet, acid smell of death in the rubble of the streets. The pleading of the dogs. The piercing eyes of the rats. How she always seemed to be thirsty.

Seeing the giant ships steaming into the harbor. The clatter and confusion of all the different languages. Fire trucks that said "FAIRFAX COUNTY, VIRGINIA," the honey-toned drawl of the women and men inside. The sharp, staccato voices of search-and-rescue crews with "NEW YORK" stenciled on the backs of their shirts, a nurse wearing a blue baseball cap with a red "C" just like Sammy Sosa barking out orders in tones as flat as the Midwestern plains that later surrounded her big city home.

Sometimes her memory would have long stretches of white emptiness. She'd remember the smell of the airless bus that had brought her to this new land of dancing snow. Then she'd remember nothing. If you were to ask her now how she got here—how she made it when so many thousands didn't—she'd never be able to answer. Because she really didn't know. So much of the months that followed that day in 2010 were a blank—more than a nation lost.

Now she'd often giggle when the snow came, still. There was something about snow she just didn't quite believe.

As she walked down to the water, with the icy steam from giant Lake Michigan rising, she remembered her grandmother in 2010.

When at first the earth began to tremble, the beams of the old hotel came crashing down; her grandmother lying trapped, her ancient Caribbean eyes still strong, looking head-on into the very soul of the little girl gripped by fear and saying, "Always remember, child, you were loved. *Always* remember you were loved."

Now at the shore of the lake, years later, back in her present time. She brushes snow off the bench and sits down. Today she will not be at work. Today her kids will have a substitute teacher.

A teacher. How can a woman with so many holes in her memory be a teacher?

The answer is that the drawings from the kids on her refrigerator at home, the kind notes from parents, and the smiles on the kids' faces when they come into her room in the morning, with little-kid sighs of safety, all of those things tell the story of what kind of teacher she's become.

Her, a woman who still can't remember so much.

A blast of icy wind swirls down across the beach from the north, and she digs a journal out of her pocket, and a golden pen. She remembers the music played at the remembrance ceremony this time. Strange music. Not Haitian at all. A piece called "Cavatina." There was a guitar. Soft and gentle. Something had happened when she heard it, something shifted inside her.

She looks at the pen, puts it to paper, remembers the music and begins to write. She begins to tell her story.

"My grandmother's name was Elizabeth. She wore a ring speckled with real gold. And sometimes after dinner, we'd be sitting out on the porch. I'd hear the sound of the wind in the palm trees—and she'd let me take a turn wearing that ring ... "

WHY RHYTHM?

Rhythm is what grounds a piece of music. It moves the process. Gives it a beat. The winding, arbitrary, irregular nature of work search often lacks that beat. There is no routine. No pattern. Every day brings different ways of someone saying no or not responding.

This lack of a routine gets even more difficult when the words used in work search lose their meaning. The words "*Career Center*" can mean, "here's where we ignore you." The words "we care about people" can mean virtually anything.

Without rhythm, the work search can become an aimless, floating waste of time. With rhythm comes the regular, disciplined focus of a well-organized project. But it also becomes more. Because with rhythm, as anyone who has ever stood close to a bass guitar knows, you feel the beat, the routine, and the substance of your search.

How do you use rhythm? Listen for the starts and pauses, the nervous tics in the way someone says something. You can pick up a level of meaning that goes way beyond simple words. If you really listen hard for a rhythm in any encounter you have along your work search path, you can pick up needs. Maybe the person you're listening to has some sort of need or they know someone who does. Either way, the rhythm of how they express themselves can give you a clue. Listening for rhythm in an encounter can require an exhausting level of focus. Because rhythm is rarely up-front and obvious. It's in the background. It's what keeps the song, and everything else, going.

The names in the story that follow might be familiar to you. They might not. But what's familiar to all of us is that every interaction we have has a rhythm to it. Maybe it's fast, maybe slow; maybe it's consistent, maybe not. But listening for the rhythm can be a key to discovering what's really going on as your journey unfolds.

As you listen for rhythm in everyday life, consider:

- Are there daily tasks that help you stay attuned to the rhythm in everyday life? Even simple tasks like brushing your teeth, filling a gas tank, walking down a familiar street. If you listen, can you hear a rhythm?

- Rhythm is a key element in consistency. Being able to consistently perform the tasks of the work search is of obvious importance. How can being attuned to rhythm help you become more consistent?

- Rhythm supplies grounding in the essentials of any tasks. Staying in rhythm feels like you are proceeding along well in your task. What can you do to ensure that there is rhythm in keeping your search moving forward?

THE STORY: That Bass Player

"Listen hard," I asked all ten of them sitting around the table. "What's the first thing you hear?"

"Guy playing the piano," several said at once.

"What else? Listen again."

This time the woman heard it. "There's somebody on bass," she said.

It was the first time the woman had joined the Wednesday night "Job Talk" group. They were all here for the weekly meal in the basement of the church. Job Talk was something to do while they waited for the food.

The woman was the only one who caught the bass. Layered into the piano. As if the crystal notes came from just one instrument.

"That Bill Evans on piano?" she asked.

I tried not to let the surprise light my face. "Yep. Sure is."

Four bars into the piece, and she says, "That's Scott LaFaro on bass. Paul Motian on drums."

We were in a small room off of Fellowship Hall in the basement of the church where 100 or so come inside from the streets every Wednesday night for their best warm, good-tasting, and healthy meal of the week.

The people had started gathering outside in the five o'clock winter darkness. Lining the sidewalk in front of what used to be storefronts but are now condos. There used to be a butcher shop right next door. The German immigrants making a go of it before the last Depression in the 30's and then the war. Building businesses. Raising kids. Now there are hungry people lined up in front of half-million-dollar condominiums waiting to get into the church basement.

The line gets longer each week. The people come in from the streets for that one meal an hour early just to stay warm. Kathy is the quiet angel who runs the operation with her husband Erwin and their son Jeff. Trudi, and some of the other ladies of the church serve the piping-hot delicious meal at six. Kathy makes the announcement of Job Talk as the clients file in from the street.

"Okay, if anybody wants to go in and do Job Talk with Roger, you're welcome to go into the Sunday School room over here!"

"He got jobs in there?"

"No," she answers, "just some new ways of thinking about how to get some work. Maybe sharing some stories of how you got some work."

"Sure, why not," says one guy.

"I did this last week," says another.

"This dude's alright," I see a chin waved in my direction. "He got nothing going on either."

"No shit?"

"Yeah … he ain't got no job either."

First guy to sit down at the end of the table is Jobo.

Jobo, as always, is doing everything fast. Permanently bent forward as if there was always a wind blowing hard against his frame. Teeth that had never known a dentist, scraggly beard.

All the guys lived on the street, but Jobo was the one who was really making it on the street and had been for a long, long time. Animal eyes that could spot food, spare change, or a warm place to stay from 100 yards away. Quick hands. Fought against everything the street had to offer. He had known the orange neon glow of the 4 a.m. sidewalks when everyone else had found their way home for the night and all the buses and trains ran empty. Known it for decades.

Whenever I asked a question to prompt the group to talk, Jobo was usually the first one who answered.

But not this time. This time it was the woman.

Her eyes like a memory of a long-ago smile. "Yeah, that's Scott LaFaro. They played here once. Him and Bill Evans. Paul Motian. Motian was on drums."

"You all know Mary?" Jobo nodded at the woman. "She used to sing."

That's when I remembered her. It had been four years since she'd been around. She'd come to see a small production of *Amahl and the Night Visitors* put on by a bunch of folks from the church.

It was Mary, sitting there recognizing Scott LaFaro's bass on a cold winter night, who had once provided us all with a moment of true mysterious grace at that church production of *Amahl*.

One of those moments you'll miss if you blink your eyes. Here's what happened:

A collection plate had been passed. The plate was full. It was being carried up the center aisle of the church, and just as the plate—held high above the usher's head—reached the first pew where Mary sat scrunched down on the aisle, she reached up high and gently tossed one more coin into the plate. Leaving every single soul in the room to wonder if that coin was her last.

The performers, stunned by this simplest of moves, took one more bow. I looked to the side and saw the Pastor's jaw drop. Later he said to me, "Those are the moments that keep you going." Then we all filed out into that cold winter night.

Later I learned a little more, from one of the ladies of the church, about Mary's life as a singer. Playing the small clubs of Chicago back in the day. She was a local favorite. Had a following. Then, when that ended, came the years sleeping in the park on Fullerton near Children's Memorial Hospital, taking meals at the church in that part of town.

Her singing life was over 30 years ago. A lifetime.

Now she sat here in a group of men, being the first to hear the sound of the bass.

"So why the bass?" I asked the group. "What could that possibly have to do with getting a job?"

Silence.

"Well, what does the bass do for the music?"

Silence.

"Let's listen again."

"Anyone," I asked, "know the name of the song?"

This time Jobo spoke up. "Sure, that's 'My Foolish Heart.'"

63

Then from the corner, Tim—an ancient, plodding African American man, as deliberate and thoughtful as Jobo was quick—looked up. Tim never spoke. But Tim had made it on the streets for just as long as Jobo. He didn't need to talk to get that across.

"One time I heard Oscar Peterson play that song. Him and Ray Brown."

Mary just nodded and said, "Ray Brown." Her eyes floating back to some smoky club, glasses clinking, as far away from the church basement as she could possibly be. "Ray Brown. Like Scott LaFaro. 'Cept Ray Brown lived."

Then I asked again: "Now, listen to the bass. What does it do for the music?"

"It's like some sort of story it's telling," Jobo said.

"But it's a story where nobody really knows the words." said Lab Tech Guy. Lab Tech Guy never wanted to tell anyone his name. Only that he had worked as a lab tech in the old Vienna sausage factory, doing quality control. So he never talked much either. But this time he said, "a story where nobody knows the words."

"Sure," now Jobo was on a roll. "It can help you remember the words."

"What do you mean?" I asked the group. "How can the bass help you remember the words?"

That's when Mary brought grace to the room one more time.

Hunched in the corner, still dressed in the heavy down parka that was her home against the wind—even though the room off the dining hall was very, very warm—Mary, almost whispering, said, "When I can feel the bass, I remember the words to the song." Then from deep inside the very heart of that down parka, Mary sang two lines of a classic jazz love song.

The lingering echo of her voice as a trained clear instrument prompted the thought, that winter had ended and the birds had returned. The room glowed in a deep blue holy kind of quiet for just a beat.

I then asked, "Anybody ever do something to try and get a job, and feel like you just forgot the words? You just didn't know what to do? What to say? Who to say it too? Feel like you were lost before you even started?"

Every single person around that table nodded their head. All eyes wide. Energy just buzzing across the room as the stories started to flow like they were all part of one giant electric grid.

"This one time? When I was standing in line for six hours ..."

"... And then she asked me how many babies I had ..."

"... And he told me he knew I was carrying a knife!"

Then I asked, "So what about the bass? What can the bass do? What can listening to a bass player—dead at the age of 25 in 1963, I think it was—how can the bass player help you with this?"

Jobo, as was usually the case, gave the room the answer.

"It's like the street," he said. "You can be walking down the street. Not just now when it's cold, but in summertime too. And you stop and you listen, and you just know there's gonna be trouble on the next block. You can hear it. You don't have to see nothing. You can hear it!"

"It's like that bass is beating out what will happen in your head. You don't need no words. Sometimes I can even hear a drum inside me. Beating along. Saying, 'Watch out!' The bass, the rhythm, helps you remember where you're going. The rhythm, the bass, that's the street. The floor. The part where your feet hit the street! You hear that. You keep walking."

"That ever happen to you with a job you were trying to get, Jobo?" I asked.

"Well, you know the gas station over on Addison Street and Damen Avenue? I know those guys. Two brothers, they own that place. They own lotsa places. So I'm talking to the one guy, he's talking about his brother, and he keeps telling me how I gotta make sure to do what his brother tells me to do. He keeps saying that. He keeps telling me about how his brother will be watching me real close. So the bass line I'm hearing ..."

"Yeah?"

"The bass line I'm hearing is: these two brothers. They talk a good game. But they really don't like each other very much. Now they never told me that. I just heard it in the way this one brother told the story."

"So the bass line was...?" I asked.

"The bass line was the *real* story. The truth. Didn't matter what somebody was saying. I could hear the real story. I know it sounds like crazy talk. But when I heard the real story, I got … well …"

"Confident?" I asked.

"I'm thinking you can't get no more confident, Jobo!" drawled Tim, smiling for the first time. The whole table chuckled.

Jobo smiled, and then went on. "Yeah the bass line is what made it so I knew what to do."

"What did you do?"

"Well, so just then his brother walks in and I say, for both of them, I say, so okay, every time, I finish one of the jobs, I let both of you guys know?"

"So how did that help?"

"Well, then they both said, okay, we gonna pay you."

"So you got them on the same page? Where they both wanted to pay you?"

"Yeah, the stuff the one brother was saying, it sounded alright. It was all the right words. 'Tell this. Tell that.' But neither of these guys trusted each other. I could hear the bass line running below all that. I could hear the real story. That's like what you're talking about, right?"

"Say it one more time, Jobo," I asked.

"Following the bass line means you can follow the real story."

With that, Kathy rang the dinner bell, and they all went in to eat.

WORK SEARCH HARMONY

What's a musical memory, and how can I use it to build harmony with others?

All of us have musical memories. Emotional connections made by the music to a time, place, person, or event. We remember where we were when a song played. We remember the words to songs from childhood. Music remains after much else has been forgotten.

What if there was some part of that memory that you could connect to right now? Was there a need you filled then that you could fill now? What was it?

Is your ability to fill that need, or a related need, part of your story? How?

If rhythm is the backbone of a journey, then harmony is a way to think about the relationships on the journey. How does your story connect with everyone else's? In this story, there are relationships between musicians, writers, politicians, and normal everyday people. Yet together, there is harmony. Something larger than clichéd notions of teamwork. As you read this story, think about the harmony not just in past jobs but also in every part of your life. Where did you experience harmony at its best? What can you build on to ensure that harmony becomes a real, concrete force in the story you use to find work? To do that, you'll need a clear, concise example of a time when you created some type of harmony.

As you read this story, think back and remember that example. To prompt that thinking, use these questions.

- Can you describe a place you worked where there was harmony?

- This story takes place in a large American city, but harmony can take place anywhere. What kind of place encourages harmony?

- Think about a place you worked where there was no harmony. What kind of workplace did you wish for then?

- What is it about you, specifically you that brings harmony to a workplace?

THE STORY: The Harmony Parade

Just a bit north of that long-buried apartment where Nelson Algren and Simone de Beauvoir wandered home from the corner tap on winter nights, huddled together, their steps sounding in unison on the cold sidewalk, an image of the Virgin Mary appeared on the concrete wall beneath the Kennedy Expressway where it crosses Fullerton Parkway. A water stain on the concrete.

Obdulia Delgado, the first known person to see the image, was on her way home from work at the hospital. As she drove down Fullerton beneath the Kennedy, traffic thundering above on the concrete artery connecting O'Hare Airport with the towers of downtown Chicago, she looked at the wall and immediately pulled over, snapped a picture, and fell to her knees to pray.

At a nearby train station, a tall, serene, and radiant black man carrying a battered saxophone case stepped off a train and through the railroad steps of smoke and time. He paused.

Hearing Obdulia cry, John Coltrane found his way to that underpass, knelt down next to Obdulia to lift his gleaming golden horn from its battered case, stood up tall, closed his eyes, and began with the two perfect bell-shaped notes of a piece he called "Dear Lord."

Nelson Algren heard Coltrane's tune and wandered up to have himself a look. A slight, bespectacled man, a counterpoint to the massive presence of Coltrane, Algren stood off to the side to watch the fun begin. Knowing that when he shows up, others will follow, Algren listened and he watched and thought of his own words. Writing so lyrical that the entire city drew a collective breath of amazement.

Two new Chicago wanderers, this time from the South Side, joined in underneath that bridge. Appearing first with a scowl, until somebody from the crowd that's beginning to build around that image of the Virgin shouted out, "Yo, Studs Lonnigan, that you?"

When he heard those words, James T. Farrell broke out in a crooked Irish grin, and Muddy Waters—as unlikely a companion for Farrell as you could imagine—growled out some questions about coming home to Chicago.

As Muddy Waters roared, the crowd grows even bigger. A weary wandering con man in the corner by himself, fifty-seven-year-old Harry had stumbled in from the deserted bleachers of a cold September Cubs game, his last name L-U-M tattooed in prison purple on the back of his hand. He was created by the writer Bill Brashler, who stood in a corner, arms folded, watching his character watch the growing crowd.

Just as Harry looks down again at his hand, another Chicagoan steps out of Miller's Pub underneath the El tracks on Wabash and joins the pack underneath the expressway. His belly full of beer and with more gut-level smarts about what mattered to people than the next six generations of baseball executives would ever even dream of, Bill Veeck hobbled over to join the crowd.

With Veeck now present and accounted for, it was most certainly the party.

Because in Chicago the music can be endless along with timeless, Muddy Waters yielded the stage in this street shrine to an elf of a man who reached just about as high as Coltrane's waist.

Steve Goodman looked up at Coltrane, grins, and said, "Hey, how's the weather up there?"

Over Coltrane's laughter, Goodman strummed songs of city pirates and the crowd sang along.

Then another voice soared, from the very deepest part of faith, Mahalia Jackson belting out what happens when saints start marching.

Pops Staples joined Mahalia; Mavis Staples and her sisters were all there, too; walking in the footsteps of those who came before.

All hands clapping, the music and the words resounding. That white-haired crazy man in the fedora—Saul Bellow—right in the middle of it all, writing, drawing out some grand idea he'd scribble down later at his desk in Hyde Park while the flocks of wild green parakeets blanketed the trees outside his window.

Over there. There's Royko tossing a softball, pushing out the door of the Billy Goat into the darkness of lower Wacker that melts into this same darkness underneath the bridge with the Virgin on the wall, looking for a game.

Studs Terkel walked over to Obdulia, cocked his head, and smiled.

Then he headed east, in a strange old man shuffle that's somehow young and sprightly at the very same time.

Studs Terkel walked out from underneath the Kennedy Expressway. He walked into the blinding, brilliant light of the sun rising over the lake to the east; he waved his arm, motioning us all underneath and around that bridge to follow him.

So we did.

Studs Terkel cocked an ear and grinned as he walked into that all-encompassing, flowing light of an endless new Chicago morning.

"Now this is Chicago," he says. "Listen! Can't you just hear all that music?"

CONNECTING TO ACTION

- Using the story as a way to jog your memory, think about places you've been where you experienced and felt harmony.

- Is there a piece of music that you connect with a certain job? Think back. When you recall that music, does it prompt other associations that could be useful in your search?

- What about situations you've been in where everyone seemed to be going in a different direction, and then somehow harmony was achieved? What exactly happened? What part did you play in that situation?

- Do others see you as one who brings harmony? How can that help?

- The people in the story were from many different walks of life. Have you ever experienced a situation where you worked alongside folks from different walks of life? Is that situation part of your larger work search story?

ENGAGING OTHERS IN MY SEARCH

How do you get others engaged in your work search?

Engaging others in a common task can be seen in the life's work of the great American musician Pete Seeger.

If a leader's prime task is to engage others in pursuit of a common goal, there is no better example of a leader. Perhaps Pete Seeger did not invent the sing-along, but you'd be hard pressed to find someone who did it better. What if you, like Seeger does in concert, could get everyone you encounter to "sing along" to the common goal of finding you work?

What does Seeger do that gets people to sing along? Everything in the way he presents himself to the world is like a welcome, an invitation, a greeting. Seeger doesn't tell people what to do. He asks them to join him. When he asks, everybody sings.

So as you read about this American institution, start thinking: "What do I do to get people to sing along?"

THE STORY: Getting Everyone to Sing Along

I was fifteen years old the day I met Pete Seeger.

Four thousand or so people at the grand old Auditorium Theatre in Chicago. Mesmerized by the rail-thin guy, sleeves of his flannel shirt rolled up, singing at the center of a bare stage. No one else up there but him. Somehow he made every single one of those four thousand people sing along with him.

Thirty years later I saw him sing at the Peoples Church on Lawrence Avenue in Chicago—and he still made everyone in the room sing along with him.

His own voice was almost gone. He sang just a bit. But he still made every single person sing.

Just him and a guitar or banjo. I have rolled up the sleeves of my flannel shirt ever since I saw him that first time, all those years ago.

After that long-ago concert, clutching a piece of paper signed by the advisor to the Radio Club at my high school, standing at the stage door; somehow someone actually let me follow a line of real journalists up onto the stage of the emptying Auditorium.

Standing with a crowd of about twenty surrounding Pete Seeger, who was politely answering questions. Looking out on to the oceans of empty seats, all the house lights up; it was finally my turn.

High school radio reporter, ready for his moment. Sticking out my gangly arm to shake hands with the great man. He said, "What can I do for you, young man?"

Open mouth, eyes wide, and forgetting every pre-prepared question, I stammered, "Ah ... um ... thank you, sir."

He smiled and said "Why, you're welcome."

Pete Seeger picked up his guitar case in one hand, his banjo case in the other, hopped down the steps on the side of the stage, and proceeded to walk up the center aisle toward the back of the theater.

Then, with all of us real and would-be reporters following him, Pied Piper style, he walked out the front door of the Auditorium, out into the horns blaring, neon light Chicago night, held up his guitar case to hail a cab, got in to the first one that stopped, and drove away into the darkness.

He will sing forever. But what's really amazing is that when you listen to him sing, you'll sing too.

CONNECTING TO ACTION

I once heard a very wise woman say, "If you want to know if you are a leader, turn around and see if anyone is following." Or using musical terms, see who's singing along.

- In Curt Coffman and Marcus Buckingham's classic work," First. Break all the Rules," the question that is answered perhaps more profoundly and completely than anywhere else is, "How do I *engage* others in a task?" And that is the relevant question here when it's time to connect to action.

- Can you think of examples of where you have engaged others into your work search by each of the following?

  - **Inspiring Trust.** Showing my credibility by following through, being reliable, and being able to communicate the value of my work.

  - **Displaying Fairness**. Being consistent and inclusive in how I interact with the world.

  - **Showing Pride.** Not just in the work I can do, but in all the people I can serve with that work.

  - **Showing Care.** When Pete Seeger leads the world in song, the fact that he cares and cares deeply is never in doubt. Thinking like Pete Seeger, *how will you get people to sing along?*

A BRIDGE TO WORK

Do you cringe when someone tells you to "think positive?" I do.

Positive thinking is so very easy to talk about. You already know that a "positive attitude" is the frame of mind you are supposed to have if you are to be successful at finding work. But when you're looking for work, it's hard to find something positive in the process. So this story goes above and beyond simple positive thinking. This is about the "Stockdale Paradox."

The "Stockdale Paradox" is a useful "thought tool" for anybody seeking work. Named for the former prisoner of war Admiral James Stockdale and discussed in Jim Collins's classic "*Good to Great: Why Some Companies Make the Leap ... and Others Don't.*" The paradox reflects the thought process that enabled Admiral Stockdale to survive while a prisoner. The idea is to simultaneously focus and act on two thoughts:

1. I am in a prison camp and it is horrible.

2. I will get out of here.

It was these two simultaneous thoughts that helped Admiral Stockdale survive.

Positive thinking alone did not help.

How can the "Stockdale Paradox" help prompt new thinking about your work search? And what does the Paradox have to do with music?

Music can be the emotional bridge you need to get you back and forth between Stockdale's two simultaneous thoughts. To keep both ways of thinking going at once. Sound complicated?

Not really. Music can be just what you need to keep the two simultaneous thoughts running alongside each other. To keep both ways of thinking going at once. Apply Stockdale's Paradox to work search and what you have is:

1. Work search is awful

2. I will find work.

You don't pick one or the other. You pick both. And music is the conduit that prompts you to hold and use both thoughts at once.

In this selection you'll travel through three dreamlike scenes. Dreams, or perhaps nightmares, are of course very appropriate settings for anyone involved in a work search.

In the three dreams you will see both the difficulty of the current situation and the expectation of changing it. Just like the "Stockdale Paradox." You'll also see music act as a bridge between the current situation and the next one.

As you read these vignettes, start thinking about your musical bridge to the right frame of mind for successfully finding work. In each of these three dreams, there was some piece of music that made the bridge come alive. Made it stronger. What's your musical bridge?

Not sure? Read the story of the three dreams. Then start picturing the music playing as you build your own unique bridge to the frame of mind that can prompt you to find work. Your bridge. To your result.

THE STORY: Three Winter Dreams

One

Something big and unnamable is coming. Like a train through a dark snowy night letting loose with a whistle that shakes the foundations of the whole forest. You don't know what it is, but it's coming.

You don't know where you are. You do not remember where you live. Your feet crunch the snow. The stinging wet drops scrape your face. You are invisible to random strangers passing quickly in the blinding storm. In an unknown city, you are reduced to being only two wide frightened eyes. A parent pulls their child close to stay out of your path. You pass a small house with an open window, you think about the insanity of keeping a window open in this storm. But from that window, cranked up really loudly and mixing with the snow, you hear, just for a moment, a few bars of Beethoven's "Ode to Joy." The music is such a joyful contrast to the blinding snow.

The moment you hear that music, a battered blue Plymouth, windshield wipers slapping down the snow, ambles easily over to the curb right next to you. The window cranks down, the warmth rolls out. He smiles and says, "Hey, good to see you back in town."

"Bus just came in. Rough storm, huh?" you say.

"Well, I'm glad you made it. Got everything you need? I'm on my way downtown. Can I pick anything up for you?"

"No, no, I'm fine. I can run over to the store and pick up some soup, bread, and peanut butter for dinner."

"OK," he says. "Well, then we'll see you tomorrow."

"Thanks, John."

"You bet!"

The snow lets up. You're safe.

Two

New Year's Day, just after sunrise. Around you, acres of a snowy city park are empty. Hum of traffic rumbling on the road called Lake Shore Drive that traces the line of the giant Lake Michigan's icy shoreline. Last night you and your pal caught the midnight show at a place called the Earl of Old Town.

Last night you two were misfits. Stomping your feet to keep them warm, outside in the line to get inside. Then tables jammed together, this tiny little place. The stage a few slabs of plywood six inches high above the floor. The performer is a wild, grinning elfin bundle of energetic joy—railing on that guitar until even the memory of cold is gone; he makes that room so hot. He is singing in a way that somehow makes you think you are just about ready to be in love.

His wife is at the table in front of yours. All the tables so close they touch.

Now everyone in the place joins the chorus. A song that just might be your road sign to love.

As his joy found its way into even the most frigidly cold corners of the Chicago winter night while his stay with us on earth was winding down ferociously fast, his wife turned around and said:

"Could you guys please pass the salt?"

So my pal and I could proudly remind each other, tromping happily through the snowy fields of Lincoln Park in the dark after the concert, that we got to be on salt-passing terms with the wife of that singer of joy.

Misfits no more.

Three

Again something unnamable coming. This time something very, very good is just about to happen.

From the snowy fields you step inside the conservatory.

It's like a zoo for plants. A tropical rainforest of green, moist ferns; trees winding branches under a clear glass bubble that keeps the snow and the winter and everything else outside. You've stepped from ten degrees of snowy cold into eighty degrees of steamy jungle vines.

Traveling deeper into the warmth, you find yourself knocking on the door of a kitchen. She opens the door and smiles; the smell of chocolate-chip cookies floats out. You hear a scratchy record album. Linda Ronstadt singing the song "Lovesick Blues."

Just about to be in love … could this be her?

CONNECTING TO ACTION

- The songs in each dream provided a bridge between a hard reality and the expectation of a better future. Where do you need that kind of bridge in your work search?

- Work search can be dreamlike. How could you use music to make some sense of this process that seems like a dream?

- Translate the Stockdale Paradox to your search. Use language that is as specific and concrete as you can make it. What is your present situation? Not just "I'm out of work." But the full picture. What is it that makes your situation unique? What is your desired goal? Not just "a job." Be as specific as you can.

- Is there music that can help you keep Stockdale's two thoughts going simultaneously?

PART FOUR:
COMMUNITIZING

Communitize. It's a word we made up here, simply by turning *community* into a verb. Communitizing is not networking. It is *not* going to a network lunch and standing in the corner talking to competitors about how no one has jobs. Networking all too often has a one-dimensional quality. "We are here to get jobs. That's it!"

In contrast, communitizing is multidimensional. As a member of a community, actively participating in the life of the community, your actions are multidimensional. You directly participate in working community challenges through to completion. You celebrate community joys. You interact with communities connected to your own. When one communitizes, one becomes woven into the fabric of a community—any community. *Communitize* is an action verb.

COMMUNITIZE AND YOU'LL FIND NEEDS

The more embedded in a community you become, the more you see needs. As we've said, needs, not job postings on the Internet, are what prompts work. In this section, we'll explore more deeply how to find needs.

Want to find work when there are no jobs? Stop looking for the jobs! Look for the needs.

Often, needs start out as being abstract. More like ideas. Needs like *safety*, *healing*, *power*, *communication*, or *organization*. But the more work you do within a community—the more you communitize—the more down-to-earth and real the needs become.

You start to see community needs in terms of the concrete stuff of everyday life. That stuff we all need to touch, hold in our hands, hear, smell, and get done.

Working from the inside of the community to your fullest, you are in the absolute best position to find those needs and connect them to work for you. You are embedded in the community. You are *communitizing*.

As you read the stories of communitizing, start thinking about ways you can use the practice of communitizing to find needs even when there are no jobs.

Then, consider all the additional places you could communitize. They could be business communities, but they can also be neighborhood groups, faith groups, professional or educational communities, or the crowd that hangs out down at the local tavern. It doesn't matter. Any community will work.

You'll know you are communitizing when you start thinking differently about work search. How? Listen to the stories of communitizing. Then decide how.

Remember always that your new goal is to stop looking only for jobs. Expand your search to look for needs.

COMMUNITIZING SAFETY

The Work of Filling Basic Community Needs

Picture a pyramid that showed all the needs of a community. At the base of that community would be safety. It's awfully hard to think about philosophy when you don't feel safe. So as you read this story of a soldier, let it call to mind all the other safety needs that are at the very base of any and all communities. Safety for people, things, ideas, the food we eat, and for our homes and institutions. Keeping something or someone safe is not limited to soldiers. Perhaps you keep something or someone safe right now and you've never even thought about it. Is there a safety need you could fill that would lead you to work?

As you read the story, think about these points in terms of the places where you communitize:

- The soldier is communitizing as a member of the military, but how many other places is he communitizing?

- How might intersecting communities help you find a need for work?

- How many places are you communitizing right now?

- What other places might you communitize?

- And finally---what are the safety needs of *your* community?

THE STORY: A Soldier Serves a Community

This man Chad *communitizes*. He's on the inside several communities.

First, the military. Chad does not "network" with members of the military. He already belongs. He's already on the inside of a community that serves in the name of safety.

Now, he is getting ready to leave home for his second tour of duty. This time in Afghanistan. But before he does, he writes a message to a second community. You'll see that message below. This second community goes by the name of "Cornerstone." Here is how that community came to be. In 2006, Chad was a member of a yearlong leadership development program for a large corporation. Chad was one of 25, chosen to be part of this team of high-potential leaders.

Twenty-five sterling souls with leadership practically ingrained in the DNA of all of them. This community named itself "Cornerstone."

If Chad were to read the message to Cornerstone out loud, you'd hear a quiet southern voice not unlike that of the singer James Taylor.

But if you were to listen to Chad's voice just a little bit harder, you'd also hear the same iron undercurrent of command that any soldier would hear as he or she carried out Chad's orders.

If you were to see him, you'd first see the grin. Then the eyes that miss nothing. Scrappy and slight with a core of steel. I once saw him scale up and over a twenty-foot wall in the middle of the woods as if the wall weren't even there.

Chad communitizes in the military and in Cornerstone. But it is in the context of yet another community, that central community of his family, church, friends and hometown that one can envision that day in the future when Chad will come home.

That day when the plane will land back home in his community, Little Rock, Arkansas. Chad will step out the door, he and his wife Tracy will instantaneously lock eyes, the kids will start yelling with joy, and the family will walk through the corridor of that airport, strangers will smile, several will salute, and many will break out in applause. Then the next chapter in the story of Chad's community will start. Because Chad has come home.

All of the communities, the military, Cornerstone, and the combined community of family, church and hometown, exist alongside of one another. In all of these communities, Chad is able to communicate a sense of safety and security to those around him

One reason why Chad is able to communicate the assurance of safety across all of these communities is that he has a language for communicating his strengths. He can very specifically explain the specifics of his talents.

The language of personal strengths Chad speaks of in his message to his Cornerstone community comes from author Tom Rath's book "Strengthsfinder 2.0." The Cornerstone team read that book as part of their program

As you read Chad's note to his Cornerstone Community, think about how a message of safety can touch everyone in sight when a soldier comes home safe. Think about how the way Chad describes his strengths communicates safety to anyone and everyone in all of his communities.

Finally, ask yourself, "What if I could communicate the way I could fill a safety need in my community?" It can be any kind of safety. Large or small. What if I could communicate the ways in which I can keep something or someone safe? How could that help me find work?

Chad's Letter to Cornerstone.

Hey Team,

I want to give you an update on what's going on in "The Life of Chad." As many of you will remember, I am a member of the United States Army Reserves. Back in June, my unit was put on "alert" for a possible mobilization. Then in September, it was confirmed that we would be deployed to Afghanistan for a yearlong rotation to perform "route clearance" operations.

Unless you are privy to military operations, you may not recognize what route clearance operations are … in short, we are bomb hunters.

Our mission will be to find and reduce any Improvised Explosive Device (IED) before it hurts and/or kills. By doing this we can minimize the casualties that have grown exponentially over the past few months … and make a few parents and children back in the States happy.

I tell you all this because one of my strengths is that I take my time when I think. I move carefully. Thinking before I step. Knowing that strength, I'm ready.

I am a careful person. Always aware that there are risks. In fact, I bring risks out into the open. I've always believed that life is like a minefield. So I have always walked with care. Like I said, I'm ready.

I share this as someone who finds comfort in knowing that God gives us all the talents we need to perform the missions we have in life. Does this mean we won't run into complications or fail a time or two? No. Just means that deep inside us all, we have strengths just waiting to come out.

My prayer is that as I lead my troops, I will remember my own words today and put each of my troops in the right situations to allow their strengths to complement others and ensure a safe return.

Nothing is certain in life and I don't take things for granted. I cherish all of my memories with you and hope to see/hear from you all upon my return home.

As with all things in the Army, the only "sure thing" is what you just accomplished … all else is subject to change.

I would ask your prayers for my family, especially my wife Tracy who will continue to home school our oldest three daughters. The younger two will also be at home to ensure that there are plenty of distractions during the school day. The oldest two vaguely remember me being gone to Iraq, so this will really be a new experience for all of them. Tracy still remembers the pain that goes along with a husband being gone for a yearlong deployment. I try to reassure her that I will do all within my power to ensure that all my troops return home safely … not just the one she's most fond of. But she still worries.

Thank you in advance for all of your prayers!

I look forward to hearing from each of you.

Onward,

Chad

Cornerstone (LCP 2006)

Epilogue: Chad came home safe. As did every single one of the soldiers under his command.

CONNECTING TO ACTION

- The need to keep something or someone safe runs through everyone's life. Safety in food, transportation, buildings. The safety need of keeping something clean. Where does the safety need show up in your life?

- The soldier describes his caution as strength. What strength of yours helps keep others safe?

- How does the fact that the soldier communitizes in more than one community help him?

- When the communities you belong to intersect, what are the needs that arise?

- How can your fulfillment of those needs help connect you to work?

A COMMUNITY'S CROSSROADS

There are crossroads in every community. Maybe it's a virtual crossroads online. Maybe it's a sleepy crossroads with one stoplight blowing in a dusty wind. Or any one of an infinite number of variations in between. At every crossroads comes a chance to find and fill a need that could lead you to work.

This very morning, an unemployed customer service manager has set up a hot dog stand at a busy crossroads north of Chicago, where he's selling hot dogs and handing out resumes. A pure and simple example of what it means to communitize. Completely individual. There is no self-help book that says, "Set up a hot dog stand and hand out resumes." Chances are that there won't be many other people doing the same thing. At least at his crossroads.

Yet his front-page picture on the *Chicago Sun-Times* was an ad for his resourcefulness. Over half a million people saw that he was ready to work.

So while you might not be selling hot dogs, there are crossroads in your community, too. Most likely more than one.

As you join in the story of the crossroads in this story, keep one question in mind. What are the needs you find at your crossroads?

THE STORY: A National Crossroads

Imagine the other diners' heads turning to watch when Humphrey Bogart and Lauren Bacall stopped by for dinner.

That's what happened at the Pump Room in May 1945, the day after Bogie and Bacall were married. Through the years Sinatra and Dean Martin were regulars. Sammy Davis Jr. gave a free concert for the folks in the kitchen. Phil Collins was refused service because he wasn't wearing a jacket and was so miffed he recorded an album titled *No Jacket Required*. John Belushi dug into a bowl of caviar with his hands. Led Zeppelin once bounced in for some chow. John Garfield allegedly urinated on the guest book; Judy Garland always sat in the famed Booth #1, the one where they brought the telephone to your table.

Plastered across the polished wooden walls, photographs and memories of all the stars, like a giant mosaic of entertainment royalty.

Average people went there, too.

Once, in the private banquet room of the Pump Room, the company I worked at hosted an event. The chairman of the company reached the table my friends and I were at, and I made a remark about the parade of celebrities whose pictures graced the walls. Saying that we were in very distinguished company. The chairman nodded absently. My friend Larry, perhaps thinking that the conversation wasn't as interesting as it could be, piped in with, "Yeah, and sometimes Roger likes to get dressed up like he's Judy Garland, stand outside on the front steps of the hotel, and belt out 'Somewhere Over the Rainbow'!"

The chairman looked confused, but he had other tables to meet and greet, so he moved on.

There are also private memories here. Somewhere in a plastic bin tucked in a corner of a basement is a picture of two high school sweethearts sitting at the Pump Room on a long-ago Valentine's Day. A flower on the table. Faces full of promise. No clue about how they'd bounce off each other's lives over the years and then one day just stop.

One day she called to ask if she should defrost a pound of hamburger for dinner. His response that he wouldn't be over that night. That night became every night.

But in that picture at the Pump Room crossroads, those two almost lifelong lovers dressed in their glowing finest, with a single flower on the white tablecloth, every single possibility ahead for them, those two were stars.

Just like Bogie and Bacall.

Along with everyone else who passed through this crossroads of the nation.

HEALING THE COMMUNITY

The Need for Healing Work

The need to heal is a constant in any community. So healing will always be taking place as you communitize. As you read this story of healing, let it prompt your own reflections on where you see the need for healing in your community. Consider all the different ways, above and beyond medicine, that communities can help heal.

For example:

- If you were to think of this imaginary conversation as being about healing, how does each character help heal?

- If you were asked to connect the work of anyone to healing, how might you do it? For example. If my work was to drive a truck, I might connect to healing by hauling needed supplies to the sick

- Now come the hard questions. What are the healing needs where you communitize? What work would you need to do to help fill those needs?

THE STORY: A Table at O'Rourke's

Mike Royko was at the far side of the big table in the back of the smoky old tavern on North Avenue, in Chicago just a few blocks from the lake. Head down. Scribbling in a ten-cent notebook. He didn't say anything when I told everybody at the table why I brought you here. He just listened when I told him about your rare and very treatable cancer. Royko knows that every cancer story is different. Everyone at the table knew that.

But when I told him what you did, he looked up. Nodded slightly. He said, "Every day? You're telling me that the column you write runs pretty close to every day?"

I answered for you, "Well, pretty close to it. Sometimes there are days when ..."

Royko growled, "I don't do math, Roger," then he looked at you, still scowling, and pulled in an empty chair. "C'mon over here, kid," he said to you. "You sit here."

I made the introductions around the table. Some of them you already knew. Guy whose job you took had driven all night down from Minnesota. Sat there quiet with his gangly legs crossed in front of him, pushing his glasses up the bridge of his nose.

Lot of the folks at the table you didn't know. That's Charlie over there. An old boss of mine. That's my Aunt Mavis. If you two start talking Buddhism, we could be here all night. Of course you know Roger Ebert. This is—

"This little punk," said the guy with the gold-wire glasses looking straight at me, "rips me off on a regular basis." Then he smiled and held out his hand to you. "Nelson Algren. Pleased to meet you."

"Some of these folks are pretty hard to get on the phone," I said to you. "I don't think they have e-mail where some of them are."

"Never mind e-mail, Roger," Studs Terkel said, and then began asking you questions. Each one honed like the sparkle of a diamond.

Three minutes later Studs said, "You're a healer." Studs looked at you again and said, "Tell me what it's like to heal with words."

I couldn't quote your answer. But I know you said you had to be very, very willing to reveal who you are. You had to listen to whatever went between the lines of any given song or story. Trusting the story you create to do the healing.

The conversation started there. Hard to say what everybody was drinking. Mavis had tea. I know the ginger ale was flowing. More people joined us as the night went on. Over there, a lady from Ohio who is a friend of yours.

As the November breezes swirled off the lake, the warmth of the room held promises of good times coming. As the night got deeper, you asked if I could write out directions to the place in case you ever came through town again.

That's when Ebert scrawled a little note and passed it across the table to you.

You picked it up and we both read:

"Once you've found your way to a table at O'Rourke's, you'll always be able to find your way back."

CONNECTING TO ACTION

- If you were to expand the definition of healer beyond medicine to include anyone who heals, who are the best healers you know?

- What, specifically, does one of your "healers" do differently than anyone else?

- Even if you've never thought of yourself as a healer, try to remember a time when something you did helped someone else heal. Not just medically. Heal in any way at all.

- Start thinking about the connection between healing and work. How could you make that connection mean something to you in terms of finding work?

THE RULES OF COMMUNITIZING

Every community has rules. Call them operations. Call them procedures. Formal, informal, spoken out loud, or just assumed. Even wars have "rules of engagement." In all those rules are needs. The needs could come in an infinite number of shapes and sizes. Defining the rules, communicating, measuring, enforcing. The needs would be as specific as the organization.

As you read this selection, think about the spoken and unspoken rules of the place described. What are they? As you begin to use this story:

- Pick any community you know. How can improving the "rules," or the operations, improve the community?

- What are the unspoken or assumed rules of your community?

- Could verbalizing those rules be a need? How about writing them down?

- How can you help with the unspoken rules?

- What would it take to turn your help into full or part time, paid work for you?

THE STORY: Don't Worry. We Have a Key.

The soft summer rain dinged the black plastic lids of the garbage bins in the alley behind the church as the man with the shopping cart and the battered blue Cubs hat whistled the first two bars of the jazz standard "Misty."

An evening rush hour, Damen Avenue, in Chicago. The man parks his shopping cart next to the chain-link fence. Two black labs in the yard next door bound up to investigate, barking and sniffing.

Chuck, who is explaining the job to me in the natural rhythm of one born to be a leader, says, "Now, it's okay if folks leave their shopping carts here. That cart's their home. Gotta make sure it's safe."

Chuck and I circle through the alley, back on to Grace, right on Damen, ending up at the front of the church.

"So that's it," he says. "Making sure we're good neighbors. That's really all it is."

Stepping north across the alley, the golden tones of "Misty" still reverberating for all who care to listen, Chuck and I then get to do something subversive.

To the ragged collection of blank-faced human souls splattered like the rain where the alley meets the street out back of the church, we get to say, "Hey, come on over here!"

A message that runs in direct and total opposition to what these good folks hear pretty much everywhere else they go: "Hey! Move along!"

Looking straight at one man and then the other, I say, "I'm Roger. I'm in charge of standing around. It's my specialty. You guys want to help?"

The two men guffaw. Chuck pronounces me trained for the task. He turns and goes back inside to finish preparing the meal.

Chuck had supplied me with a trash bag. So I say to my two fellow sentries, "Guys, I forgot to tell you that sometimes I just suck at standing around. Don't do it well at all. So I'm gonna walk around and pick up trash. If you see anybody in the alley or on a neighbor's front steps or yard, will you tell them, 'Hey, c'mon over here'? You know, make sure they know they're with us?"

"You a crazy man!" one of the men smiles.

"Sometimes I am good at standing around. Sometimes I just can't!" I wave, walking away, bending down to pluck out an empty potato chip wrapper from under the rosebush and stuff it in my litter bag.

The rain picks up just a little. Still light. It sweeps that soft melody of "Misty" into a puddle where the alley meets the street.

Floating down the parkway on Damen Avenue, somehow still fluttering despite the rain and the music, a napkin never used. I grab it just before it lands on the wet grass.

In grabbing the napkin, in the rain, hearing "Misty," I am back at my first holy meal.

It's at a Burger King.

Mr. McDonnell was presiding. We were all carefully spreading napkins on the orange-and-tan plastic seats bolted to the floor. My sister and I, Mrs. McDonnell, Spencer, Eric, and Ian. Spencer is around 10. Like me. In later years, I would be proud to be called "the other McDonnell brother."

We had just left the church. Now it was time for our best meal of the week. I can taste the salt of the fries to this day. Right now.

Back in the present drizzle on Damen, I pick up the last of the litter; ask my two new friends if they're going to help other folks stand around. They say they'll work on it. I go down into the church basement to see if there's anything I can do to help before my next turn at standing around outside.

Inside, the meal is just about to begin, so I go up and motion my two fellow sentries inside.

Downstairs, the room is filled with purpose. A lot of hungry people. A quiet dignity. Order. There are rules in this room where people wait to eat. Unspoken rules. But they blanket the room in a calm comfort that is as different from the street as can be.

Order. Rules. They aren't always fun. They are rarely as gentle as they are in this room with the rain whistling Erroll Garner's "Misty" gently on the windows.

Mr. McDonnell had rules.

Back during one of the times I lived in the McDonnell basement, kept warm in the most brutal Chicago snows by a friendly, ancient boiler, I was truly surprised and schooled by one of the rules. It arose in preparing for a visit from Laura.

Laura, a long pressed-blond haired, blue-eyed daughter of a Rhode Island doctor, was a "friend."

What that meant, back as the closing days of the 1960s stretched on to the early 1980s, was that you put the word "friend" in air quotes. Then you'd say, "No, really. We're really just friends."

But you'd silently wish otherwise.

I was so infatuated that had somebody told me she liked to put baby kittens in sacks and twirl them around her head, I would have made up a reason why that was okay. So a visit from Laura was a big deal.

Seeing that the McDonnell's' house was small, I volunteered to sleep on the floor for her visit. Right next to my bed. Where Laura would sleep.

But there were rules. So, that sleeping arrangement of course never happened. Thanks to Mr. McDonnell.

I remember his greeting Laura as if she were royalty. All through the visit he was as nice, Mrs. McDonnell might say, "as pie." No one could have been nicer. But of course there were rules.

Back to right now in the church basement, I had been given the word that one big rule was to stay out of the kitchen. "It gets too crazy in there," I was told.

So as I bend down to peer through the serving counters and into the kitchen, I ask, "Kathy, I'm watching the alley outside tonight, but it's pretty quiet. Anything I can help you with here?"

"Sure," says Kathy, who is running the show with Chuck. "We might be short a server. Hang on a second, we're almost ready to go."

As I watch, I see the kind of operation that comes when every silver cylinder of a gleaming proud machine is firing full speed ahead. Henry Ford did not design an assembly line that worked this well.

Trudi, smiling as always, and the crew now serving the good stuff. The warmth of this food just reverberating off the walls in the same dignified way that the man in the alley whistling "Misty" had blended right in to the music of the rain.

The service now done, and the meal now in crescendo; everyone was eating.

I went back outside in the soft rain to make my rounds again. No stray souls in the alley or the yards. No one on the front steps along Damen Avenue.

Turning the corner in front of the church. Sitting in the front seat, passenger side, of a car with an Oklahoma plate, door open, and his legs splayed out in the gutter, sunglasses and a porkpie hat in the rain.

Staring up at a tree branch and mumbling. A mixture of serious, angry, and confused across his face. In my mind, his name was Monk.

I said to Monk, "You eat yet?"

He answered in a mumble that said Caribbean more than Oklahoma.

"I am looking at the branches of the tree."

Then he starts into a monologue where no one word seemed to have a relationship to the one that came before it. When he finally draws a breath, I say, "Are you hungry?"

He answers with an angry bubbling West Indian diatribe that I think ended with, "I am not a shoemaker!"

Chuck comes out to take a quick break and greets the man with the immediate respect and honor of the street. Something communicated that is way beyond words.

But the man keeps rambling. We listen and nod for a moment or two. Then Chuck says, "We have to get back inside."

The Caribbean Monk's words suddenly become clear. "Wait! Come back! Don't go!"

Chuck answers matter-of-factly. "We got work here. I'm sorry. We don't have time for this."

As Chuck and I walked back inside, he says, "That's a lot of rum he's had tonight. Maybe rock cocaine." Shaking his head. "Out of control. Too bad."

Later, back outside the church in the soft rain on Damen, Mark—from church—walks up. He is escorting the now-quiet Monk downstairs for some food. In communities, some people can get through to others and some just can't.

"Hey, how's it going?" I ask. "What are you doing here tonight?"

"Oh, I just thought I'd stop by, see how things were going."

Mark takes the quiet Monk downstairs as the sounds of Ruth's piano come drifting out to the rain-soaked street. Then Mark walks back outside and we just stand and chat. About everything and nothing.

Back in the alley, even as the rain slows down, a small gust of wind blows the church door closed, and it automatically locks.

"Uh-oh," I say. "How will we get back in?"

"Don't worry," says Mark. "We have a key."

CONNECTING TO ACTION

- The story takes place in two different time periods. In several different places. Yet each place and time has rules. Both spoken and unspoken. Making the rules, engaging people to live by the rules, changing the rules, all of that takes work. Yet, it is part of every community. How can you, as someone who communitizes, connect yourself to the *work of making rules work?*

- Rules are often seen as negatives. If your communitizing were to spark rules that made the community better, cheaper, or more efficient to manage, could filling that need add some sort of value? Could that value mean work for you? How?

COMMUNITIZING INTEGRITY

Doing What You Say You Will Do

Filling the need for integrity in a community can be described as a very abstract principle.

Or, it can be as clear and direct as doing what you say you will do.

In this story, filling the need for integrity isn't about preaching or moralizing. It's about doing something. Without that, there would be no communitizing. Use this story as a tool to recall times when you have done what you said you would do. In other words, acted with integrity. Then ask yourself:

- If integrity means, "doing what you say you will do," how would you describe an integrity need someplace where you communitize?

- What could you do to fill that need?

- How might filling that need connect you with work?

THE STORY: Eating Our Dessert First

He can't speak Greek. So the second I got the e-mail in Greek from him, I picked up the phone and called.

"Why did you send me an e-mail in Greek?"

"What are you talking about, Roger?"

"I just got an e-mail from you. It was sent to me and a bunch of other people. It was in Greek."

"Wait a minute. I didn't send you an e-mail. I'm not even on my computer."

"Well, you better go look. Maybe it's identity theft. Somebody is sending e-mails from your account. That could be serious!"

He started to laugh. I knew the laugh well. Countless days through almost a decade of building a business. In books they'd call him a mentor. In real life, you'd call him, oh I don't know, I'll use the name Paul. If I were to use the word *mentor*, he'd probably say something like, "What the fuck is a mentor?"

He kept laughing. But I was thinking, can't be too careful about privacy. Lots of people have been hurt by Internet piracy. Millions of dollars stolen. This was serious. Why was he laughing?

"Let's see here," he said as he sat down at his computer. I might have heard a grandkid in the background. It was the cocktail hour. I do know the sound of a Manhattan swirling over the ice. "Look at this," he said. "There's a message that went out that I didn't send. Hmm. How about that."

As he looked through his e-mails I remembered that day in the big hotel ballroom. Somewhere in Florida, or maybe Dallas. Big trade-show convention rooms all look the same. We were standing at the double doors in the back. Three or four hundred people watching the PowerPoint presentation in front. The guy in charge of getting all our customers was there in the back with us. My job was to keep those customers. Paul was the boss. In our march across the country to make sure our software replaced our competitors', we were up against a company literally 10 times our size.

By the time we were done, at the end of the nineties, we had taken 75% of the market. That's starting with zero. Thousands and thousands of customers. We hung on to about 96% of them, too.

But back in that big hotel meeting room, back when we were just starting, I remember what happened when those double doors opened up and two hand trucks wheeled in all the trade-secret training and product specifications of our competitor's. All of it. Totally confidential information that belonged to our competitor.

I looked at the boxes. Looked at him. I said, "What do you want me to do?"

Never will I forget what happened next. He looked at me. Looked at the boxes. Looked at me again and said, "Get 'em out of here. Don't even open a box. I don't want to win that way."

Turns out we *did* win, without opening those boxes. When we were done with the job, at the end of the nineties, he left the company and made it possible for me to leave as well. Possible for me to go start my own company. To know the pressure and the relief of making payroll myself.

Then he went on to some other businesses. Operated the same way he did the day he told me to get rid of those boxes. Worked hard. Did everything he was supposed to do to have a calm, financially secure retirement. Always working to win the right way.

Then the recession hit. In those times of hardship for everyone, he lost all of it. No complaints. Didn't ask anybody for anything. Did nothing wrong. He lost it all.

So when I called him up worried that somebody could steal his identity on his computer, he just started laughing and said, "Roger, after what we've gone through? If somebody wants to mess with my computer, I'd tell 'em to have a great day. I got nothing left to steal."

Then I started laughing too and said, "Good point."

"Really," he answered, "it's something that makes you kind of stronger, believe it or not. I ain't saying it's good. It ain't good. I wouldn't recommend it to anyone. In fact it's pretty bad. But when it comes to things like somebody messing with my computer? I don't worry about stuff like that. I tell 'em, have a great day."

He talked about his kids and grandkids. Taking care of his mother-in-law. The new place they were moving into. His wife was over at the new place with painters. Asked in detail about what I was doing.

I asked how his wife was doing.

He said, "Well, you know we were talking about it the other day. We have a lot of memories. A lot of memories. The kids, the grandkids, the family. She said to me, "You know Paul, I guess we just got to eat our dessert first."

I was quiet. Then I repeated it. "You got to eat your dessert first. I don't think I've ever heard it said better than that."

"Hmm," he answered.

"I really like that line. You got to eat your dessert first. That might be true of a whole lot of people. Do you mind if I write about this?"

"Go ahead, Roger," he laughed. "Have a great day."

CONNECTING TO ACTION

- Remembering that integrity is not just a concept, it is also practical, real-world action, which integrity needs in your communities are called to mind by this story?

- In this story, Paul led an organization that reflected his integrity. An organization—like any community—can be formal or informal. If there is integrity need to be filled or fixed, usually more than one person has to be involved. So the question then becomes, "How have you—or how could you—engage other people in fixing the need?"

- What kind of value would that fix be to the community?

- How could you include the story of how you fixed that need in your search for work?

- What could be different if you did include the real life story of how you acted with integrity in your work search?

Check Out Receipt

Sulzer Regional

Wednesday, June 14, 2017
11:34:39 AM

Item: R0500393610
Title: Finding work when there are
no jobs : stop networking, tell your
story, start thinking differently
Due: 07/05/2017

Total items: 1

Thank You!

791

PART FIVE:
SOLVING A MYSTERY

Ever solve a problem, perform a task, or figure something out that was just baffling to someone else? Congratulations. You solved a mystery.

You didn't know it was a mystery. You thought you were just hanging a picture on a wall perfectly straight. Making a cup of espresso. Painting a fence without spilling a drop. Or filling a copy machine you'd never seen before with paper. *But to someone else, it was a mystery.*

Solving someone else's mystery can give you a connection to work. Simply because you can do something that someone else can't do. Or perhaps doesn't want to do.

The challenge with these kinds of mysteries is that you will not normally notice them because to you they are not mysteries!

In each of the stories there is a mystery being solved. Use these stories to get you thinking about your own mysteries, where you provide the solution, give the clue, answer the call. Mysteries, like communities, always contain needs. As we keep saying, it's those needs that light your own individual path to work.

HIDDEN MYSTERIES

Because mysteries are hard to see when they are only mysteries to other people, we will start with what we call a "hidden mystery."

In the course of this story, a boss reveals a mystery. A mystery he says he does not know how to solve. One that was also new to the employee. What happens next? The boss fires the employee.

This prompts a whole new set of needs on the employee's part. Chief among them, finding work.

But it also prompts a new thought on the part of the employee. "What if I can solve this new and previously 'hidden' mystery? Could my solution lead me to a new work?"

Solving mysteries can be tough at any time. In times of crisis, like job loss, solving a mystery is even tougher. The need to solve a mystery takes a backseat to needs like paying for food.

As you read this story, let it lead you to your own situation. Are there mysteries you can solve that have been "hidden" behind more immediate needs? If there are, can solving those hidden mysteries help you on the path to finding work?

THE STORY: Why Was I Fired?

Speeding north on Lake Shore Drive at 10:30 on a bright winter-sun morning. Lake Michigan anchoring the world to my right in a swirling white blast of arctic cold. Probably shouldn't be taking a cab moments after I got fired.

But I was, as Led Zeppelin once sang, dazed and confused.

It was January. Subzero winds whipped through Chicago. But twenty minutes before I was warm and much more protected on the twenty-second floor of the downtown office tower, the comfortable offices of the small consulting firm where I thought I'd be talking to my boss about plans for the year.

I say talk. He was on a video monitor. Broadcasting from southern California. Palm trees swaying behind the video screen shot of the short man with a deep voice sitting behind the gleaming, totally empty teak desk that made it impossible to tell whether his feet actually touched the floor. The consigliore of the family that ruled the company; in the six to eight months I had reported to him, I had only spoken to the guy in person once for about half an hour, in southern California. I speculated to myself that the deep voice on the phone was a bit affected—but the conversations only came about once a month and lasted only for seconds. A terse two- or three-word e-mail every week or so. So all I had was speculation. I really didn't know the guy and he'd never done or said anything negative to me—so I didn't really have much to go on. Until that day he fired me.

He was actually really nice that day. Said it wasn't working out. Said he was sure I'd find something better. The longest and nicest conversation I ever had with the guy. Then he said this:

"Bill, everywhere I go in the company, people like you."

I thought instinctually: well, apparently not everywhere. I'm being fired because people like me?

One thing I did hear a lot from others was that this guy would never make a decision like this on his own. Somewhere, there was a "Judas" in the corporate crowd. Later I found out whom, but that's the boring part of the story.

Here's the interesting part. It was what he said next. He continued:

"And after people tell me that they like you, they say—and really I heard this a lot—they say, that Bill, he really makes me think."

He then wrapped it up with: "And I think they're right. You make people think. Frankly … I don't know what to do with that."

So I was being fired for making people think?

A few hours later found me sitting around a table with our pastor and my wife. All of us stunned, scared, and angry. As that immediate reaction faded, gratitude took its place. Golden waves of gratitude for all the support I had begun to receive from virtually ever corner of my life.

But back in that taxicab, right after I got the word from the little man on the video screen, I remember mulling over that line, "You make people think, and I don't know what to do with that." I remember rolling it out in my mind, swirling it around, dipping it in the waters of the frozen inland sea to my right, taking it out, and looking at it again and thinking:

Maybe he just told me an absolute truth.

I do make people think. Even more, I have a need to do that. I love doing that. That's what good teachers, coaches, and writers do. He doesn't know what to do with that. To him, it's a mystery.

But maybe I do know what to do with that. What if I could solve that mystery?

CONNECTING TO ACTION

- First, a quick review. What was the hidden mystery here? It was the perception that the narrator made people think. That perception was new to the narrator. Not once had he ever even thought about making people think. Or that it might someday be a factor in getting fired. But, like many mysteries, there was more to the story. The boss did not know what to do with someone who made people think.

- Connect this story to action by first recalling hidden mysteries in your own life. Hidden mysteries are tough. They can be mixtures of irrationality, surprise, fear, or anything else.

- Now comes the interesting part of this exercise. Ask yourself, *"What if I could solve this mystery?"* Think about the story. The narrator swept aside everything but the question that had sprung from the hidden mystery and asked, *"What if* I could do something with making people think?" How could you take a similar approach?

- And finally, lets say you did figure out how to solve your hidden mystery. *How would you connect your solution to finding work?*

PURE CHANCE

The Mystery of the Chance Encounter

Chance encounters always carry the hint of mystery. But can chance encounters really help you find work?

Think about the organized, measurable, defined process of the job search line at the beginning of the book. Remember how empty it was. How it did not work for you.

Now consider the chance encounter. Especially chance encounters in the places you regularly communitize. What if you were ready to turn a chance encounter into work? What would you need to do to make yourself ready?

In this chance encounter pay attention to the questions one character asks another. What if the answers to those questions had been known? Could those answers have prompted a new path to finding work?

THE STORY: A Dairy Queen Night

Walk a few more blocks east on Grace Street after dinner, in the sweltering August night humidity, and you're at Dairy Queen.

Dairy Queen forever connecting the tall grass cricket sounds of a country road with the neon city glow on the very same night.

She picks the malt. Me? The chocolate chip mint. Not even a thought about what kind of chemicals they use to make this stuff. Because it tastes so damn good.

Approaching the counter, she says to the girl standing behind the register, "You're Samantha, right? Samantha Ryan? From church?"

"Oh yeah, I used to go to church."

"We saw your confirmation ceremony."

"Yeah, I made a deal with my Mom. If I finished that, then I didn't have to go anymore."

"Yeah," I said. "We don't go much anymore either."

So we paid for the ice cream and left to see the sights on a Monday night. As we walk back out into the summer night, she says to me, "Samantha's Dad, he sure was a great cook, wasn't he? I wonder how business is going at that restaurant of his?"

We strolled past the outdoor place where people were packed in eating juicy blood-red slabs of red meat and drinking heavy red wine on the sidewalk at 9:00 on a Monday night.

Next came the old theater. The old movie palace where a guy plays the organ. Then a Thai place. All of them bustling with people.

"What did her Mom do?" I asked.

"You know her Mom. Works in human resources for one of the big stores downtown."

"Oh, of course! I wonder how she's doing? I wonder if she still goes to church?"

"Or if she's like those of us that didn't fit the mold," she answered.

"Those of us who were a little bit different than the rest," I said. Then we were quiet for a while. Walking home. Liking that Dairy Queen.

Back home and cranking up the air conditioning.

"Think I'll write for a while," I said.

She was standing on the stairs. Looking up at me sitting in front of the computer.

"Remember how long it's been since we got to take that walk to Dairy Queen?"

"Three or four months. Most of the summer. Pretty cool that you can walk again."

"Four months," she said. "April 25th. That's when I went on crutches. Next day I tried to work, tried to teach dance to thirty 3-year-olds. And I can't believe all the get-well cards I got from parents! I have addresses from what, 200 people now? I wonder if that mailing list will ever come in handy?"

"Mmm, yeah, I wonder what you could do with a mailing list like that?"

"A mailing list and now we get to walk to Dairy Queen."

"And look who we see? Somebody from the church we don't go to anymore."

"So what do you suppose that means?" she asked.

"Beats me. But did it seem to you that there were a lot more people on that walk than you, me, and a kid from our old church?"

CONNECTING TO ACTION

- Most of the questions asked by the characters in the story were about people not in the story. People who were a mystery. Could any of those mystery people provide a lead to finding work?

- Has there been a chance encounter in your life that is worthy of reflection and follow-up? One that could lead to work?

- Who would you most like to encounter by chance? What's the part they would play in connecting you to work?

- What can you do to make sure you are prepared for a chance encounter that could lead to work?

GIVING TO GET WORK

How can giving lead to finding work? That sounds like a mystery.

Thinking about giving at a time when you need work might initially seem like the most ridiculous idea you've ever heard. Giving? You are scraping to make ends meet right now! Now is not the time for a moral judgment about it being better to give than to receive. Now is the time when dinner matters more.

But as we have seen tine and time again, work search is often not rational.

Putting "Giving" in the context of work search can bring unexpected results. Perhaps even mysterious results.

In this story, the narrator hears a message telling him, very simply, to give something … and it makes no sense to him. But at the end of the story, he receives. The story connects the mystery of giving to the mystery of receiving.

So as you read the strange story of the mystery oranges, try to figure out the mystery here and then answer the question, "What did the storyteller receive?"

When you're done, we'll come back and talk about what in heavens name that has to do with finding work!

THE STORY: Mystery Oranges!

"Give oranges," said the voice.

I looked up from addressing Christmas cards at our dining room table. No one else in the room. It was a gray, cold Sunday afternoon. My wife was lost in a frenzy of baking. She bakes the way Michelangelo painted the ceiling of the Sistine Chapel.

Christmas music filled the house and fueled her every motion. The football game played without sound as the Chicago Bears played without heart.

"Give oranges," I heard again.

"Honey, I've got to get something upstairs," I shouted into the kitchen as she danced from the stove to the sink.

After climbing the stairs and walking into my closet where all the important stuff that wouldn't fit anywhere else was tossed in a big white plastic bin, I pulled out the yellow envelope and slipped out the death certificate.

January 12, 2007. Yep. My Aunt Mavis the Buddhist was still dead.

It had been years. Still sometimes I checked. Especially when I heard a voice saying things I didn't understand. Like, "give oranges."

It was usually her.

Walking back downstairs and looking out the front window at the tiny bare tree on Grace Street where I could sometimes feel her presence, I remembered a Zen koan. One of those stories that demand a second read before it even begins to make sense. She loved those kinds of stories.

The Zen Koan

One day as Manjusri stood outside the gate, the Buddha called to him, "Manjusri, Manjusri, why do you not enter?" Manjusri replied, "I do not see myself as outside. Why enter?"

I heard Mavis laugh and clap her hands with delight and then recognized her voice saying once more, "Give oranges!"

Walking into the kitchen, I pulled off the shelf a book that I bought just after she died. *The Seat of the Soul*. It was by the author of *The Dancing Wu Li Masters*, Gary Zukav, one of Mavis's favorites. I bought the book thinking about how I'd never get to talk to her about it. Then put it on the shelf, unopened.

I opened it. It had been long enough.

What if, the book said, there were more than the five senses we humans use to make sense of the world?

Imagine how good that orange would taste. Tossing up the orange and catching it, I could see and touch its skin. Shaking it up next to my ear I could hear a faint sloshing. A taste like a thousand summer nights. The smell was heavenly. But that's only five senses. What if there were more?

What if a multisensory person could expand the channels through which they take in the world? What if my personal frame of reference somehow grew to the size of a blue and endless Montana sky?

Then I heard her say again, "Give oranges!" I still didn't understand.

I walked into the kitchen where my wife was unraveling dough like an ancient rabbi rolling out a Torah.

"Well, this year didn't turn out like we planned," I said. "Turns out the world didn't change in a year."

"Does the world ever change in a year?" she asked.

"Probably not," I answered. "But I sure wish we could buy each other all sorts of cool Christmas presents. I wish we could take that trip up north."

"I know. But we're making it. We'll get by. We have everything we need."

"I think what I want for Christmas is an orange," I proclaimed.

She's used to hearing things like that. It's been almost 15 years now. So she just smiled and said, "Okay!" Then she went back to her baking and I went back to the dining room to finish up the Christmas cards.

I sat down, and as I picked up the pen I heard Mavis say, "Finish much writing lately?"

"No."

"And the reason?"

"Mavis," I said, "I don't even know the next time I'll see a paycheck! I don't know if my wife and I will be living in our car 6 months from now!"

"Do you have a story to share right now?"

"You mean besides hearing a dead person's voice saying, 'give oranges'?"

That's when I heard her laugh the loudest. I looked outside and it had begun to snow in Chicago. A gentle snow that stilled the troubled ground.

"Okay," I said, "I'll finish the story. But maybe we could talk about it when I'm done? Maybe if you just told me where I could find you? Where you'll be?"

Mavis answered, "Remember Steinbeck's story? Remember what Tom Joad said to his mother when she asked him that question?"

"I sure do. She told him that she'd be right there with him in all the treasured moments of everyday life. Course Steinbeck wrote it much more beautiful than that."

"That's where I'll be," she said.

"So what do I do now?"

"Finish the story."

"Then give oranges, Roger. Just keep giving oranges."

CONNECTING TO ACTION

Work search normally starts with the question, "How can I get?" What could change for you if work search also included the question, "What can I give?"

What did the character here get when he heard the mysterious voice saying, "Give oranges?" He got a connection to a loved one who had passed away, motivation to finish some written work, and a different way of thinking about how to experience the world. You could probably find a few more things that he received. What does that suggest about you thinking differently about "giving?"

Imagine expertise as a gift that can be simply given. It can be expertise in anything. For example, imagine the expert baker of chocolate-chip cookies who has never had a bakery job in his life. He puts that expertise into action. Bakes the cookies. Gives them to a bakery and talks to the owner. What if his cookies were better than the ones already in the bakery? What could that gift help him get?

Now start thinking about the infinite ways that expertise can lead to work. As you go about your daily business of work search, find out about the expertise you see in the people you meet. Ask them, "How did you end up doing this work?"

As you listen to the answers, try and find the part of the story where someone *gave* something to someone else.

THE GATEKEEPER MYSTERY

Who's a Real Expert?

This story prompts the question, "Do we sometimes let our notions of who is in charge and why they are in charge get in the way of finding work?"

Ever listen to an expert speak on any given subject and then think, "I already knew that," or "That's just common sense," or maybe even "Where do I sign up to be an expert? Because I can do that." Or did you ever run into a gatekeeper? Someone whose job is simply to tell you "no"?

Use this story to question your own assumptions about expertise and gatekeepers during the work search.

How have gatekeepers gotten in your way?

THE STORY: The Resume Expert

Maybe you've met Kristie? Hard charging and practically hardwired to her smartphone. A very nice, polite, and sharp young human resources rep. She is a "resume expert."

That means that she's in charge of screening resumes. Which means that in a world where finding work when there are no jobs is the new reality, if you are anywhere north of fifty (forty in certain industries), she is in charge of telling you "no." No one ever told her to do that. She learned from passing resumes from people of all ages up the ladder to hiring managers. More often than not, the hiring managers would say things like "a little heavy on experience." So Kristie soon got the message.

If Kristie were to Google *ageism* (which of course she never would), she'd find solid research going back to 2006 citing ageism as a bigger barrier to employment than sexism or racism.

If, on the other hand, she were to visit her parents one night, maybe on a Wednesday when nothing else was happening, and Dad was laughing at a rerun of a show called *Seinfeld*, perhaps she'd see a guy dressed in white standing behind a cafeteria steam table making up hard-ass rules about who will receive some of his delicious soup. Before Kristie could quickly scamper out of the room so her Dad wouldn't ask her to watch, she might hear the character called the Soup Nazi bark out, "No soup for you!"

Kristie would never see what she had in common with the Soup Nazi. He had a steam table and she had a "do not reply" e-mail message. But their cry to the world sounded awfully similar.

Kristie's cry is: *"No job for you, Grandma!"*

Of course, Kristie isn't the real problem. She's only what's most visible in an era when preferring someone less experienced for a job has become commonplace. Spread out behind and around Kristie is a complex web of economic market forces, HR departments with a mission to defend the status quo rather than find and grow talent, and a societal tidal wave of indifference that lets ageism happen with barely a peep.

Why? Often it's because ageism is very hard to see. Take a look at an ad that appeared on a national job board this morning. See if you can find the ageism.

Organization Change Management Resource – Chicago, IL

I have another need for an Organizational Change Management resource. As many of you will recall from the last few times I have sourced for this type of person, the candidates being presented were all OVER qualified. So, following is the information that I provided to you all when sourcing previously for this role.

Basic Description:

This role provides change management and communications support for complex projects and organizational changes. This position will support the OCM Lead and Program Effectiveness Lead and collaborate with various support resources to deliver tightly integrated and effective change management plans.

This is not a leadership role. They will not have anyone reporting to them. Need a doer with three to four years of experience. Resource will be taking direction and guidance from the lead, but they need to be independent and not wait to be told what to do.

For those of you who don't speak corporate, here's a translation:

Listen up, you old guys and gals! Yeah, you. You know who you are. I told you this once. But you didn't get it. Slow, huh? Trouble HEARING maybe? I guess I need to write LOUDER. So now I will tell you again in the exact same way. You're the ones who used to have jobs because you were experienced! Well, we don't need ANY of that here! If you have ANY more than three years of experience doing this job—forget you, Sam! You will take direction. You will not have direct reports. You will be a DOER! I'm not even looking for a person. I am looking for a RESOURCE!

Ageism is illegal. Just like racism and sexism. To top it all off, ageism doesn't have to be limited to folks over forty. It can be a factor in blocking younger folks from work as well. A way to tell a person that there age is the wrong age for the job.

Still another piece of this giant pie is that being a "fit" for a job can be real criteria. Or it can be an excuse for ageism.

Most importantly, ageism, like sexism and racism, is a systemic problem. It's more than Kristie. It's a system. A larger web of interlocking bells and whistles. Kristie has power because the mysterious people behind the gates she is guarding, *want* her to have power.

Of course Kristie doesn't have to worry about any of that. She's the resume expert.

She's in charge.

CONNECTING TO ACTION

- Kristie's job is to guard her system. If you have stood in the job search line we talked about at the beginning of the book, you've already met Kristie. Locked up tight in a mysterious room behind Kristie could be racism, ageism, sexism, so-called experts and shadow figures wanting only to keep that system watered and fed. As you think back on your work search, what other obstacles have you encountered that could be part of a larger system?

- Kristie's system can easily feel all consuming to anyone seeking work. So much so, that another mystery is given little or no attention. *That mystery is, what are the real needs of this place where I am looking for work?*

- In thinking differently about finding work, what if you started down the road of solving that mystery? Not the mystery of Kristie's system. The mystery of what an employer really needs. Going beyond a job description. Instead, finding out directly from someone who would know, what a place needs. Will this be an easy task? No it won't. It's a mystery. But think what would happen if you solved this mystery!

SOLVING MISTREATMENT MYSTERIES

When a business, or any organization, is mistreating its employees in any way, or when there is even a perception of employee mistreatment, then there is a need.

No employer I know of ever wakes up in the morning, stretches, gropes for that first cup of coffee and thinks, "Gosh, I can't wait to go to work and do someone harm today."

But it happens. Employers do mismanage, abuse and even steal from employees. Wage theft, employers stealing from employees, has been estimated to be a $3 billion dollar a year problem.

As you read this selection, ask yourself, "Where have I seen any kind of employee mistreatment? And how could I use the fixing of that problem as a springboard for finding work?" Or even more broadly:

"Can fixing something in a workplace help me get more work?"

THE STORY: A Mistreated Employee

When Mary first saw the problem, the big mystery was, "How could anyone do this to someone else?"

When she pulled the email off the printer at 5:30 on a Friday evening, telling her that she had been fired, she had no idea that she was now part of the $56.4 million dollar a week problem of wage theft across the United States.

Those of you who still have pay stubs, have you busted out the calculator and made sure everything was there that should be?

You might want to.

A recent, massive study of wage theft, underwritten by four independent foundations, using a validated sample of 4,387 workers across the country, found that the typical low wage worker lost $51 a week through wage violations.

Mary came out ahead. She was told, in a three-line email from her employer of four years that the $15 that was missing from her paycheck would be mailed to her. That she need not return to work.

She knew she was taking a chance, a few days earlier, when she communicated the fact that the check was short $15.00. She feared she might be fired. Then she was.

The national study, "Broken Laws, Unprotected Workers" cites that only one in five workers communicated their wage issue to their employer. I'm guessing that very few of that 20% did so the way Mary did. Wage issues can be viewed, especially by those who don't have them, as "he said–she said" problems requiring the delicate untangling of the trained human resources professional. Most stories have at least two sides.

But in Mary's mystery of the missing $15.00, there was no dispute about whether she was owed the money. Only over whether she'd be paid for her work. That was the real mystery.

So when she documented that the employer was welcome to keep the $15.00 and she would only have to consider other options if this practice of not paying her what she was owed became a regular event, she knew she was taking a chance. But, as she wrote to the employer, she liked her job. Seeing that there were no other issues over the previous four years, she hoped to continue.

Her case was strikingly simple. She wasn't paid.

The national study reports that victims of wage theft cut across all ethnic and racial lines. Although wage theft was once almost always limited to companies with less than 100 people, that's no longer true. Most victims are women. The occupation hardest hit by violations?

Those, like Mary, who work with children.

The research, the most comprehensive undertaken in the past decade, paints a grim picture. Not just in the morality of how we as a country stomp on the dreams of those at the low end of the pay scale. But also in the economic enormity of the theft. Hard data showed $56.4 million dollars was stolen from the paychecks of Americans by employers. Without getting lost in the numbers, that figure comes from estimates that 1,114,074 workers in New York, Chicago, and Los Angeles alone have at least one wage violation per week.

Every single week.

Money that could have been spent on food or health insurance or shoes. Money stolen so regularly that it becomes a way of life.

Payroll—like health insurance policies, telephone charges, and credit card rates—can get complicated.

But sometimes issues are not complicated. They are very simple. Someone works for an agreed-upon amount and the employer decides not to pay them. That's it.

Mary ended up getting the $15.00 but loosing her job. So no one stole from her.

This time.

CONNECTING TO ACTION

- In thinking about this story, start considering what it would mean to your work search if you started reframing employer-generated problems as needs. A tricky tactic. One that must be approached with care. Because as you saw in the story, there are some mysteries that employers don't want solved. But there are also employers who *do* want their self-generated problems solved. How will you tell the difference?

- Is there an example of such a mystery—an employer-generated problem—in your life? What would it take for you to solve that problem?

- If you did, how could your solution lead to work for you?

PART SIX:
PRACTICING STEWARDSHIP

To practice stewardship is to take care of something larger than you. It's the final principle in the search for work. Final because in some way or another, it encompasses or touches all of the principles.

In every one of the previous stories, we've seen ideas. As we've traveled further and further away from the regimented, cookie-cutter approach to work search, we've put those ideas in different settings so they can prompt you to toss them around, try them on for size, make them yours, and then finally prompt you to circle back and apply them to the work of finding work.

The primary vehicle for putting those ideas into action is your story. Every time an idea is added to your story, your story gets stronger. Strong stories are what get you closer and closer to work.

Music, community, and mysteries, like stewardship, give you ways to organize those ideas. To hold on to them. To let you form, juggle, and continually improve the ways you put them into action to find work.

While music, community, and mystery are all bigger than any one of us, when we start talking about stewardship, we rise to an even higher level of abstraction. One can hear a piece of music, see a guitar, live in a community, and solve a mystery. But the ideas we're using to paint our picture of practicing stewardship are even more all encompassing. They are even larger. Ideas like "unity," or "caring," or "completion."

Think of these ideas as dimensions of what it means to practice stewardship. As we put these dimensions of stewardship into a story, something truly amazing starts to become clear. A clarity that could perhaps be life changing.

When we start seeing these ideas in real, concrete terms of a story, we find that they speak to the very heart of work itself! What work does not require unity? Where can you find a job where you don't have to care? Who is it that gets paid for *not* completing work? What becomes clear is that these big-picture ideas are the real heart of finding work when there are no jobs.

So as you travel through these stories of practicing stewardship, let them take you even further away from the land of slicker resumes and job interview tips than you ever imagined you'd go. Let the stories take you to the full glorious scope of what it means to practice stewardship. Let the stories take you up into the blue-sky wonder and allow you to look down on yourself while you search for work. Only this time, this time it will be different. This time you won't be standing in any line. This time you'll be able to look down and see the full scope of needs that come when you start practicing stewardship. You'll be able to see exactly how you are going to go about finding work when there are no jobs.

We'll start with "unity."

CAN UNITY PROMPT WORK?

What's Practical about Unity?

Practicing stewardship sounds like a very abstract, head-in-the-clouds activity. One that would bend more to the poetic than the practical.

Finding work, on the other hand, means action. So, how to you align the poetry with the action? Let's start with just one "big picture" idea and show it in action. Let's start with unity.

Unity is a great place to start because it's always needed. Although unity is a sociological and even religious idea, it also has a lot to do with very pragmatic, work-related questions, such as, "How do you get people who don't like each other to sit in a room long enough to get something done?"

As you read this selection on unity, look for those concrete, practical questions sparked by the story. As always, those are the questions that lead you to needs. If you were to think back to a situation where you had to do the work of unifying a group of people, what did you do? What was the result?

After reading this story, the key question to consider is, "Could your talent or experience in unifying people or even things be part of the story you tell in your search for work?"

THE STORY: Dr. King's Toss

I was 8 years old when Dr. King came to speak in our village.

Dr. Martin Luther King Jr. still had about three more years of work to do before he'd be shot on the balcony of a motel in Memphis. Gunshots that would set angry fires blazing and police sirens wailing pain in almost every big city in America and then land him squarely in the history books forever.

But before that day, he spoke in our village. It was really different from anywhere else he had ever done his work.

He spoke in the Village Green, a square block of open green near the downtown section of town. Nothing even close to this had ever happened here before. The population of the village was 13,000. By day's end, the crowd to just see him was put at 10,000.

I keep calling it a "village."

Back when Dr. King spoke, you could almost call it a village. Just 100 years earlier, it was a general store on an Indian trail. A sprinkling of cabins in the woods next to the giant, wild Lake Michigan.

Today the town is just another suburb where kids—and some (but not many) kids of color—drive their own BMWs and Mercedes to high school.

But back when Dr. King spoke, it still echoed the small-town village it once was. The town square that day could have been lifted straight from a Frank Capra movie, with Jimmy Stewart coming home from the war as the featured speaker. Not the Reverend Dr. Martin Luther King.

There wasn't a lot of talking in our family as we walked to the green. My Uncle Frank, a true New Deal, Adlai Stevenson supporter, an intellectual guy who was a college administrator and an old-line liberal Chicago Democrat who had earned a Purple Heart in World War II, did most of the talking. Uncle Frank was pretty excited. So was my Mom.

My Dad, with his crew cut, was often mistaken for a CIA agent when my parents went to antiwar rallies. He was quiet, preferring to wait for facts.

I was a skinny, big-headed kid with a crew cut, in a wide-striped T-shirt tossing a baseball who looked a little like an extra on the set of the TV show *Leave It to Beaver*.

So because this was a place that felt like a small town and because I've always had a curiosity about the way things work, after we got to the green and my Mom put down a blanket, it was no surprise when I said, "I'm going to go look around." My Mom said, "Make sure you're back before he starts to speak."

The afternoon had started to build to a sort of cautious festival feeling. There were folk singers and a warm-up speaker or two, all of whom Uncle Frank had talked about or knew. The crowd was building steadily.

Perfect for the little stripe-shirted storytelling boy to go practice something he still does: being invisible.

Quiet children who don't want to be seen have ways of blending into the background so that even the most observant of adults would have to do a double take to make sure they saw a kid.

That's what I did.

Being invisible does not mean being still. "Still" prompts suspicion.

So what I would do to keep moving but still stay invisible was toss my baseball up to about face level and let it plop down in my mitt. All the grown-ups would see the baseball, but I was invisible. I could watch and hear everything they said.

Up near the front of the crowd, behind the podium and microphone, was where I felt drawn. A thicker, deeper crowd there. Easier to get lost. More policemen than I had ever seen, so it had to be safe. My Dad and Mom wouldn't mind.

Everyone seemed to be waiting for him. For Martin Luther King. Everyone said the name as if it were all one word: *martinlutherking*.

I stayed in the middle of all this, waiting, part of the crowd. The longer I stayed and the more invisible I became, the more I began to hear a word repeated I hadn't heard at all from Uncle Frank on the walk to the big show.

I'd catch the word at the end of a sentence, because the emotion of the sentence was put on the one word. The word was *arrogant*. I thought I knew what it meant. But I didn't hear the word a lot so I wasn't sure.

I'd hear the word laden with some sort of emotion. Then I'd see the same kind of look my parents would give each other when they wanted to communicate something unpleasant without using words. That knowing arch of the eyebrow.

"Arrogant."

I might have even heard somebody say "uppity." That, I understood.

I was about to go back to our family blanket when I saw the cars. The cars held me riveted. There were seven of them. All the biggest, blackest, shiniest Cadillac limousines; bigger than any car I'd ever seen driven by the rich people who lived on Sheridan Road. My eyes went round—cars were almost as interesting as baseball. I knew I was supposed to be back with my parents (I was a kid who pretty much did what he was told), so I knew I probably should go back. But these were really cool cars! I could slip back through the crowd like lightning once this enormous parade of black metal rolled to a stop. I could not get my little eight-year-old brain wrapped around the questions: "Why does martinlutherking need so many cars? How did he get so many cars? Which car is he in?"

The cars rolled to a stop. What happened next held me in absolute awe. Out of each car came a parade of large black men, all dressed in the sharpest suits I had ever seen, looking everywhere. Scanning everything. Every face. Every sound, every nuance of movement. I had never, ever seen that kind of attention to anything.

Still as a rock now, the only movement the toss of my baseball, I had my very first moment of sheer, overwhelming, breath-stopping, heart-pounding, stomach-tightening panic: when I realized that these terrifyingly focused men were coming straight toward me in a wedge formation.

I was standing right between this rolling thunder of men in suits and the microphone. I wondered what it would feel like to die.

With the first battalion of this group of men three steps away (they were not moving fast; they were being very, very cautious as their eyes scanned the crowd), with the first man so close I could see the jagged shape of the red handkerchief in his breast pocket, I understood what these men were doing.

They were looking around like that—staying so close together, never smiling—because all 20 or 100 or however many had gotten out of those cars were protecting someone.

They were guarding the man in the middle. The one I could see now. The one who looked so tired. I looked at that man and even I could see: that man is very, very tired. I remember thinking, "I wonder if he'll take a nap when he gets home like my Dad likes to do sometimes on Sunday afternoons." It did not occur to me at that instant that the man was martinlutherking. I was too scared for a thought that rational.

Just then my fear ratcheted up to yet another level that was totally new when I realized that the man in the middle of all this, whoever that man was, had actually seen me! He looked right at me! He looked right at me!

About six steps away. I was frozen. Even the baseball was hidden in the mitt.

The man at the very center of all this put up his right hand. His palm in my line of vision. Framed against an open, blue summer sky. As he did this, as he raised his palm, everyone around him stopped moving! They just stopped. Right there. Like he had pulled some sort of magical brake that held them all.

Then that man with those bone-tired eyes looked at me in a way that told me he had kids, too.

Could that be how "arrogant" people look at kids? I sure didn't think so. Of course, I was only eight.

While all those men in suits kept looking everywhere, surrounding him, protecting him, he said to me, "You play ball, son?"

I nodded. Speech had totally left me.

Then he held out his hand, the one that that had stopped the parade, and said, "Son. Give me the ball."

I nodded. Handed it to him. He took it. Rubbed it in his hands, the same way I did, the players did, the same way anybody would. He closed his tired eyes for just a minute, and I saw the faint lines of a smile when he said, "Got to make some time to play some catch."

Then he tossed the ball back to me.

Thank God I caught it.

CONNECTING TO ACTION

- Unifying a group often starts with one personal connection. The little boy walked into a situation that made a personal connection possible. How often, do you go to a place that makes a personal connection possible? Could doing it more often help your search?

- The people in this story were not unified. Yet there was a tiny moment of unity between the man and the boy in the toss of the baseball. Think back to situations you've been in where disunity has prevailed, and then somehow, there was a tiny moment of unity. *What did you do that helped trigger that tiny moment?*

- How do you transfer or connect what you did in that *tiny moment* to some other group that needs unity?

- What are the groups in your life where there is a need for unity?

- How will you include the way you promote unity in your work search story?

THE WORK OF CARING

Can Caring Connect to Work?

Caring can be so easily marginalized in the search for work. Swept under a carpet of clichés like "find the job that gives you passion." When clichés like that one appear, the meaning of the words themselves are lost.

Caring has also been crushed by the weight of putting food on the table. What everyone cares about is making enough money to live.

So true caring for others gets lost. When that happens, the work search road grows cold. Because caring is like a fuel for thinking differently about finding work. When you care, you are including whoever or whatever you care about. So you're never alone. That loneliness we talked about at the beginning of the book is gone.

What everyone does not always have at their fingertips is a definition of what they're supposed to care about as it pertains to the search for work. Because of course you care about a lot of things. They can easily all get jumbled together. Hard to define. Hard to know what to include as you tell your story.

So as you journey through this next story of a lifetime of solid, dependable, and unwavering caring, start thinking about the real-world acts of caring in your life. What does caring look like? How does caring connect to a need?

In this story, the caring spans generations. Caring is bigger than any one person. So caring is a dimension of stewardship. Caring lasts.

This story also, like an earlier piece, centers on the woman we will call Aunt Mavis. Note the very practical concrete ways that Aunt Mavis showed she cared. Then ask yourself, "How do I translate my caring into action?" *Perhaps even action that could lead me to the work of caring.*

THE STORY: A Life of Caring

Sometimes in the comforting gray late-summer light that holds the Chicago Loop in a subdued humid hum of pure power, I can feel the presence of my grandfather, Frank J. Dowd. Gone since I was just a kid. A red-faced, weary, knowing smile, wisps of white hair, round and good to his grandson, suspender-popping Irishman.

Strolling down Randolph or LaSalle Streets, his spirit sings in the summer gray shadows cast by the crisscrossing of the massive steel and concrete pillars that hold firm and strong the El trains rumbling above as they endlessly circle downtown Chicago.

Feeling his presence, I wonder if heaven is anything like Chicago. I imagine him leading quite the large and motley crew of a welcoming party for his youngest, Mavis (who died several seasons ago, in the absolute frigid, bitter and barren cold of a January day), but before that, helped raise me and make me who I am.

My grandfather steps back, with a wink and a smile, to let Mavis on through. She has just a few questions for both Jesus and the Buddha. She'd like to get this afterlife thing settled once and for all. That, and then get on to the next set of questions. She will have many. She will include everyone in the conversation.

While she asks questions and keeps the party going, I look back. Searching for the scattered drops of water that splash from the river, her life always full and flowing forward.

I'm seventeen again. On the coffee table in the living room of Mavis's rented townhouse north of Chicago, where I lived in the basement for a while, there is a paperback she'd been reading lying open. Lurid, splashy dime-novel colors on the front. *The Last Picture Show.* An author named Larry McMurtry. "Hmm," I remember thinking. Larry McMurtry. "I wonder who he is? I wonder if I'd like him?"

A lifetime later I do. What he wrote opened up reading for me as an adult.

If my Mom taught me to play the A, E, C, D, and F chords on the guitar to get me started, Mavis would have taught me the seventh chords. The chords that sounded cool. Mavis taught me a song by Phil Ochs called "Changes." First cool folk song that I could ever play myself. More would come.

Thinking of how Mavis cared, the giant smiling voice of the great Chicago folk singer Bob Gibson and his big 12-string guitar rings out. I can hear him singing right now. An echo like a smile that lives forever.

Steve Goodman listened to Bob Gibson and became Steve Goodman. Roger McGuinn listened and became the Byrds. Jeff Tweedy listened and is still listening today ... so the music is alive right now. I started listening because Mavis did.

Stories heard in bits and pieces from other rooms, filtered through the lens of a kid who didn't know that much yet: sure Mavis met Tommy Makem, she knew the Clancy Brothers, she loved to ride horses, there was some connection to actually riding in the Olympics.

Mavis lived first in Libertyville, which was then a distant outpost in the wilderness. With Uncle John, who was a real live Indian! Along with a great big and bounding German shepherd named Little Bear.

Then there was a small house somewhere off the expressway. Mavis, now with just Cousins John and Mike, moved into a small apartment in a not so nice part of town. But in that apartment, there were hand-painted designs on the bright and cheery kitchen walls and an honest-to-God very cool Mexican guy named Hector who always seemed to be there. Mavis had a blue Chevy Impala, a car much cooler than our practical and reliable VW bus. When Mavis took care of us, she always went nuts cooking us all the bacon we could ever want for breakfast in the morning. Imagine endless strips of bacon!

Living in apartments decorated with blue Mexican glass, guitars, and bright Mexican throw rugs and wall coverings, Mavis worked in politics, for the Democratic Party. Mavis was and always would be a teacher. She started a conversation in Spanish that never stopped, and I could always see the amazement at her pitch-perfect accent and fluency on peoples' faces.

I never understood the language, but what I always did understand was that whatever mistake I made in my life, chances were that Mavis had already made it.

What that did for me was beyond any kind of measure and sat squarely in the realm of poems, stories, and song.

A marriage came to an end for me, and Mavis understood. She had been there before.

I can remember standing in the street outside the stately red brick house with my Dad and Uncle John as we came to help Mavis move out of the house where she had spent the brief months of her second marriage. I can remember my Dad and Uncle John smiling the knowing smiles of men who knew of life and marriage and men and women. Though I didn't know way back then what all that meant, I knew while standing in that circle of men outside Mavis's house I would be thinking of my Dad's and Uncle's smiles until the day when their meanings would come clear.

Then another red brick house, just west of the big Northwestern football stadium where Mavis lived with her third husband, Dick, who gave me, as a very young guy stepping from teaching into business, the single best piece of advice for getting along in business that I have ever heard. I was frustrated by circles of power that I didn't understand in a big corporation; Dick said to me, "Roger, it's not that you're wrong. It's that you aren't the vice president in charge!"

I can remember a winter night in the big house Mavis shared with Dick. John and Mike were gone somewhere and I was spending the night in the very warm and comfortable basement. A soft show blanketed the streets and a local park where there was a slight bump of a hill. So we went skiing. Remember: this was the suburbs of Chicago. Not a lot of hills.

My first time on skis. Mavis and Dick laughing on either side of me, pulling me up Mount Evanston, a gradual bump maybe six to ten feet high, and then me whooping down the three-second slope doing commentary on the danger of it all.

That scene in the snow changes to a summer day when Mavis, John, Mike, and I were at one of the first glass-recycling sites, where it was actually possible to throw and let shatter against the side of the giant bin any and all glass jars and bottles.

So John, Mike, and I started screaming things like: "And THIS is for all you DID to me!" Then whipping the bottle at the wall to watch it burst and shatter. "You even TOOK THE DOG WHEN YOU LEFT!" Lines and taunts and outbursts that would have been great lyrics to a bad country song. While Mavis just laughed uproariously thinking all three of us very, very, funny.

I can remember walking through the old Wieboldts in Evanston, the soft hum of the old department store, and I started improvising a commentary on the clothes that I would pick up and display for my audience of Mavis and Dick, who again simply could not stop laughing.

Through Mavis, I learned I could be funny.

Growing up a funny fashion commentator, throwing glass bottles at a recycling bin, skier of tiny bumps in the road.

Then one day when I finally did find the love of my life, I told Mavis.

And she believed me.

I saw Mavis last in December of 2006. Another upstairs apartment. She had assembled those of us who came after her: sons, grandsons, granddaughters, daughters in law, nieces and nephews. Somewhere there are pictures. She made sure there was a camera. The time that night was short, because she didn't have much time left. Mom had been there to take care of her and had done everything humanly possible. But time was running out.

A few weeks later she called on a cold winter day to say good-bye. She said to me, "It's been a long road for us, Rog. Over fifty years. A long, long, road."

She told me about the day she was taking care of my brother and sisters when my parents were at the hospital and I was being operated on in a potentially life-ending procedure. She remembered how my parents looked when they walked in the door at home that night. "I had never in my life," she told me "seen your Mom or Dad look that bad. I thought for sure you were gone. You were the first. You were here before John and Mike were here. If you were gone, I don't know what I would have done."

In her words, in her saying good-bye, in looking back now, I think how loved I was.

Mavis died on January 12, 2007. A bitter cold, sunshine-bright winter day in Chicago. I had walked to Lincoln Avenue to get the newspapers. Coming back and thinking about going to visit her in the hospice.

My wife met me at the door of our house saying, "Michael called." I said, "She's gone." My wife nodded yes.

Mavis was very clear about not wanting a funeral.

Mavis's son and granddaughters scattered her ashes into the Pacific off the coast of San Diego, where they can forever float on down to Mexico and Costa Rica and soar on off to the Far East, to lands of Buddhist temples, and maybe even drift back here to Chicago.

A few weeks after she died, the cold still blasting its icy grip on the city, my wife and I ventured out at night to a ballet. The wind was overwhelming. The cold all-encompassing. I realized we were walking down the street past the hospice where Mavis had died.

Just then, at that moment, the wind got even colder. Cold beyond belief. Through my teary frozen eyes, I looked to my right and saw we were walking past the Newberry Library.

A historical library where they keep lots of old maps.

With thoughts of those maps, I could see Mavis's spirit soar up and out and over that hospice and into the Newberry Library. Just to look at maps. She would love it! In front of that library, a park once known as Bughouse Square, where socialists once stood to make speeches. She would stop for a moment.

Then in the golden, orange autumn leaves of October, the park benches full of people eating lunch and reading the great works of time, feeling the warm breezes of autumn, basking in the shimmering promises of the flowing October light, she'd always come back. Every year in October, she'd come back.

So, it's in those warm autumn breezes of a golden October that I expect Mavis will stop for a moment. Back from traveling. Mavis will come back, sit down next to me on one of those benches. Tell me what she's learned from talking to both Jesus and the Buddha. Once again in that golden autumn light, I will be loved.

I am bathed in the golden warm glowing light of autumn that shimmers off every inch of that park in front of the Newberry Library. Even now. In the last days of summer.

Mavis is traveling. Off on a trip.

But she'll stop back when I need her.

CONNECTING TO ACTION

- How do you show you care? Of course it depends. But if a person were to look at a picture of you caring about something, what would they see? Perhaps you'd be listening? Showing attention to detail? Solving problems?

- How do you include that picture of the way you care in the way you tell your work search story?

- How can the fact that you show you care lead you to work? Tough question. It will require some thought. Everyone's answer will be different.

STEWARDSHIP IN ACTION

What Does a Steward Do?

Perhaps you've met someone who has the ability to just know and act in ways that are true and lasting. Someone who goes beyond just being smart. You might see them as being smart in ways that matter.

True wisdom has a timeless quality.

Above all, the person with wisdom does not live in a vacuum. Being so aware of the world around them, the person with wisdom can be more aware of needs than anyone else.

The wise person can be stewardship come to life.

So as you read this story, ask yourself, what does stewardship in action look like? Where do I know wisdom or stewardship in my life? Most importantly, how can a wise person I actually know help me find the needs that will lead me to work?

The answers will be different for every person. What will remain the same is the last question: "How can wise people I actually know help me find the needs that will lead me to work?"

THE STORY: When the Women Took Charge

Around the time Brenda died, an entire section of a street collapsed just north of the church. An underground water main burst, the concrete crumbled, the trees and cars and fire hydrants started sinking into the earth, water gushed out in torrents into the 10-below wind chill winter night flooding the world—as if the ground itself was gone and there was no place left to walk.

That collapse of the very earth, that literal shaking of the foundations, didn't even begin to paint the picture of what it felt like to lose her. Because this was Brenda.

Comforting words of faith sat dimly lit on the sides of the frigid waters of the street where there was no place to walk. The words weren't kicking in this time. Dim lights on the sidelines just not taking hold. Because this was Brenda.

In this past week of sleepless nights and drifting minds since she died, sometimes I'd be doing something like driving down the street, and just for a second I'd have to force myself to focus on things like the steering wheel, the turn signal, or the brake. Not really sure, I'd be thinking, if I could find the words to describe this loss. Even if I could, why would I have the audacity to say them out loud or write them down?

A late afternoon gray winter sky enveloping all of us, I let myself into the church. Standing alone in front of the alter she had taken care of for so very, very long, I thought again about the audacity of even talking about her and what she brought to our community.

Then I heard her voice.

In those same strong, clipped Welsh tones, I heard her say: "Don't be ridiculous, Roger. Say your piece. Say it clearly. Say it with faith for all. Then be done with it!"

As I heard her voice, I closed my eyes and I could see her. Smiling eyes of wisdom and God's love. A twinkle, then a laugh. Right there. In the pews about halfway to the back. I could see her sitting there. There she was!

I have never known such a leader.

She'd bristle at the word *leader*, I am sure. But I'd say it anyway and that part she would like. I remember the time I caused some ripples in the church by partnering with a local group of another faith to let them rent a part of our building. Brenda called me one night to get to the bottom of it all. She did things directly. She hadn't liked what she'd heard in the arguments around this dispute.

I will never forget Brenda saying to me about halfway through the ninety-minute conversation, "All right, Roger. I can't believe I'm changing my mind, but you're right." At a church meeting we had a week or so later, Brenda got up to speak in favor of the partnership. Her husband Noel, in one of his most brilliant moments—and there have been a lot of them—kicked the ball into the net by standing up, simply reading our church's "welcome" statement printed weekly in our bulletin, and then sitting down without saying another word.

The moments come pouring in: Brenda in the basement rec room, holding court for me and a few other folks. Noel walks up grinning, gives her a crisp military salute, and says, "Permission to speak!"

Because this was Brenda. I remember her leadership, her command, but I mostly remember a lot of laughter. A lot of laughter.

Just last Sunday; I sought her out as she came into church. My wife was down with a cold and wouldn't be able to be there that morning to hear Brenda speak. So I passed along my wife's deepest apologies.

Brenda replied, "Missing my talk is not important. How she's feeling is important. I'm coming over after church to see how she is!" So that—because this is Brenda—was that.

When she got up to speak, this always elegant, true lady got behind the podium, reached up to pull down the microphone, fumbled with it a moment, and said, "I'm just a little girl." Our temporary pastor jumped up instantaneously to step up and help her. But before the pastor had taken two steps, Brenda had of course fixed it on her own.

No one knew that it would be her last message to her community.

She spoke of her childhood. Her village back in Wales. Then she began to talk about coming of age in the early days of World War II.

She paused for a moment to remember, and then she said, "Then all the men left, so the women took charge."

Imagine all she summed up with that one line.

Her full message that day truly was a miracle. I'm sure as I remember it again and again through the years, I will be as fed with the spirit as I was the first time I heard it. It was as if she had opened history's gate and let gently flow a history of faith from little village churches in the mountains of Wales to the flat bustling streets of Chicago. She made our history blend with everyone's history. Brenda gently reminded us that like everything else in the greater story of those who have faith, all of this has happened before. She told us that the church, her community, had been there for her.

In leaving the gathering that morning, I remember feeling a head held high and a renewed strength while walking behind her. She told all of us, she told me, that we could weather any storm. She told us we'd be fine. She told us not to worry.

Forty-eight hours later she was gone.

In celebrating her life and moving quickly and efficiently—as she would have wanted—to heal from the body blow this faith community had taken in losing this force of a woman who kept us all strong, I can imagine an almost endless soothing rushing stream of Brenda stories. Years from now, children not yet born will see holiday decorations that new hands unpack from an old wooden crate every Christmas, and they will hear stories of Brenda.

This is what will happen through the years:

In the room built by Brenda and Noel right off the front of the church, a pastor will pause before walking out to lead the community. She will take a drink of water from the faucet in that sink installed by Brenda and Noel. Somehow she will be able to speak of loving a neighbor, as she never has before. Speak of love in a way that every single thirsty soul in the community will hear.

Or a blessed bride and groom will stand and wait to be married exactly as my wife and I did. Lay a hand on the counter. Then they will be blessed with a marriage that is filled with love supreme.

All of this beginning in the room built by Brenda and Noel.

By simply placing their hands on that counter, somehow, some way in that place where faith is made real, they will feel the message of the great theologian Paul Tillich, and they will know and maybe even hear a voice saying:

"You are accepted! You are accepted by that which is greater than you and the name of which you do not know. Do not seek for anything, do not do anything, do not intend for anything. Simply accept the fact that you are accepted." Believers, questioners, questioning believers. All of us.

That's what we do here. We welcome.

No matter where on life's sometimes weary and often joyous journey they are right now, people will touch that counter, walk to the front of a loving community of faith, no matter who they are. They will be accepted.

They will be welcomed and told we are glad they are here.

We can do that here. Those who come after us can do it too.

Because Brenda showed us how.

CONNECTING TO ACTION

- As you reflect on the story, start looking for places, institutions, businesses, organizations, and social causes in which the leadership dimensions of stewardship might come into play.

- Now find the leaders. Official or unofficial. The people you can look at and say, "Here is a person with true wisdom." In this story, Brenda was an unofficial leader. Her authority came from the way she lived her life. Her stewardship of the faith community was a big part of that authority. Don't look for people with titles. Look for people who are true leaders.

- Once you've found the leaders, start asking them about needs of that place. Maybe it's obvious. Maybe it's not. Maybe you need to figure out how to put the need into words.

- What are the connections between those needs and finding you work?

THE LEGACY OF STEWARDSHIP

When the Five Principles are really working at their peak, they often blend together. Or combinations of the five blend together. Practicing stewardship often springs from communitizing. Because when one is an ultimate steward, when one leaves a legacy of stewardship, it's because of the way they took care of a community. As in this story about a man who left a legacy of stewardship by taking care of the vulnerable.

In his case, huge numbers of the vulnerable.

THE STORY: The Ultimate Steward

A gray splattering summer rain settles in over Chicago the morning that brought news that Senator Edward Kennedy had passed. Rolling down Grace Street, right outside my window, a wheelchair-bound man glided smoothly down into the street and up the other side without breaking rhythm or a sweat.

See that sidewalk? The way it's made with no curb? Before the Americans with Disabilities Act championed by Senator Edward Kennedy, they didn't make sidewalks like that.

Listen to this phrase: "Every major piece of social legislation over the last 30 years." If it was something that helped those least able to help themselves, he had a hand in it.

That was after they shot his brothers.

So as a chapter in American history snapped shut and historians started totaling up all the ways he helped to make a better world, I wonder for just a moment how they'll count the times somebody in a wheelchair glides across the street without breaking rhythm.

I imagine his final days, being taken out to the ocean to gaze at the water, feel the wind, and reach for the sky.

Next to that booming ocean, on the soft green rolling grassy fields of forever, he joins in spirit all those brothers and sisters that he hasn't seen in so very long. They are running. Tossing a football. There is laughter like you've never heard. Laughter melting into tears and then back to laughter as they run.

It's as if you can almost hear a faraway voice sing, of summers gone and pipes calling. Calling out to absent friends.

You think: even now, there is always time for one more song.

A song from a place where people take care of something larger than themselves. They take care of each other.

CONNECTING TO ACTION

- Think back to a time when you took care of someone or something that was vulnerable. How were you "practicing stewardship"?

- Accessible sidewalks for wheelchair-bound people is practicing stewardship at its most pragmatic and concrete. What other pragmatic examples of practicing stewardship have you known?

- What was the work that went into those examples?

- Does that work offer a hint or a clue to how you could find a need for a pragmatic way to practice stewardship?

- How can you convert that need into work for you?

COLLECTING AHA MOMENTS

Can Aha Moments Help Us Connect to Work?

They are those tiny rare moments when you know that something very important has just happened. You might not know why it is important. You might not understand all of it. But you know for certain that something important has just happened. We'll call them Aha Moments.

Remember that Aha Moments can come from anything. You might have painted 10,000 walls. But that one wall you painted, the one that was featured in the newspaper because of the way it helped keep the sunlight shining inside the factory and helped improve worker morale, that's the wall you talk about to anyone who could help connect you to work. The second you finished painting *that* wall was the second you had an Aha Moment.

In reading this story, think back over your work life for those moments of value when you made the most of your time. Not the six years you spent working for Acme Industries. Think of the moment in that late afternoon meeting when you had an idea, said something, made something, convinced someone—and then everything changed. Don't look for world-shaking, cancer-curing events. Most of us don't have them! Look for the moments when you used the time you had to its fullest. That's an Aha Moment.

This story takes place at a wedding because weddings can be times of great personal reflection and also times for looking back.

Remember that Aha Moments can happen anywhere.

When have they happened to you?

And of course an Aha Moment can lead us to answering our most important question. What is it in that Aha Moment that might lead you to some sort of need—the kind of need that could prompt work?

THE STORY: The Aha Moments of Life

Running through cool sand under 2:00 a.m. starry skies, clothes tossed along the way, splashing into the sea, then diving under the waves and coming up laughing shivering joy.

Was that us?

Not this time.

Aunts and uncles, moms and dads, families you were born to, families you choose, all tucked away in the borrowed beach house rooms along the Jersey shore while the kids raced the sands and rode the waves.

Once it was us. Crashing the waves or traipsing big city neon streets or even standing in your very own kitchen polishing off a bottle of really good tequila.

Aunts and uncles, be they genetic or chosen, know these moments well. Aunts and uncles receive the rewards of the sprint. Those crystal sparkling moments of sprinting top speed certain you will stretch, leap, and fly across the finish line first.

Parents get the rewards of the marathon. The long, slow, steady climb of achievement, reaching for strength you didn't know you had as you lope along behind the kid, shocked and so proud that she saw that hole in the road and leaped across it before the shouted warning even left your mouth.

What happens at the wedding is that both the sprint and the marathon race toward a finish line together. Two kinds of time converge. The exuberance of the end of a golden sprint. The deep quiet pride of the marathon well-done.

Seems like just a moment ago it started.

Now I stand on my sister's porch, listening through the window, and hear my once-tiny nephew, now a six-foot-tall groom, say to my father, "Bud, would you like me to help you carry that luggage?" Of course my father answers, "No, no, thanks Ben. I've got it."

Ben answers, "Well, I'm going to help you anyway."

Just like that: the little boy is gone. Somehow in his place, a man.

Ben and his fiancé came together while traveling in India. In tiny villages, along quiet roads where there are no tourists. In teeming, ancient cities he once heard her laughter inside a building. Circling Asia, they later found other times and places where their paths had almost crossed again while circling Asia, he told me. Places they stayed where they would both look out separate windows and see the exact same view.

Brides are the stars of any wedding. But this one kicked it up a notch.

The invitation was her freehand drawing of every single wedding guest. Drawings she did from photographs. The night it arrived at our house, I opened it up and thought, "That's nice." Then my wife said, "Wait a minute. Look at this. That's us! Sitting at that table!" We then proceeded to study this tiny masterpiece for half an hour. Ben had hand-scripted names to fold over each face or figure, so there was even a program to identify all the players.

Uncles keep a respectful distance. Both in watching the preparation for the ceremony in the church across the street and at the wedding itself.

Watching this bride glide from Korean flower arranging to the preparation of the Indian food. Then suddenly Ben would walk by and she'd jump on his back and off they'd go laughing like two smiling young trees in the wind.

A snapshot at the wedding dinner. The ninety-year-old matriarch, Ben's English grandmother, sits with Sokyo's mother, Mrs. Kim. Neither speaks the other's language. But they talk and smile, pat each other's arm, laugh and nod their heads. Then, the bride sees them talking from across the room, walks through the crowd, kneels down between the two women from different ends of the earth, holds both their hands, and translates.

At the cake cutting, the bride doesn't just make sure her husband's face is covered with cake; she cuts pieces and plasters them all over the faces of each of her bridesmaids in another explosion of laughter.

Then another gift to every single person in the room. All the bridesmaids and the bride's mother, Mrs. Kim get up and sing a traditional Korean folk song. There is no need at all for translation. The sweet lilting harmony cascading like a waterfall joining the world. Just a sweet song of joy.

The next day brings Ben riding a bicycle in the late summer sun, waving, saying, "Guess I best get to the bank or pack or something. We're going to Peru tomorrow."

That night, there is pizza and Mrs. Kim cooking up something that simply tastes like it could sustain a person's very soul. I dish myself some from the bowl on the table, and she shakes her head a vigorous "no!" Pulls me over, digs into the bowl with her chopsticks, and gives me three times as much; then she smiles and nods her head quickly, as do I.

The bridesmaids, Mrs. Kim, and Sokyo present Ben's grandmother with some small decorative Korean art. "Grandmum," says Ben, "this is paper made the way it was made a thousand years ago."

Then they sing the song a cappella again. This time the words are passed around, and I remember the first line:

It is no accident that we meet.

That night the airport runs to Newark and JFK begin. Giant white whale international airliners arcing up into higher skies bound for Heathrow and Manchester and Seoul. Snappy little domestic flights bound for Chicago and North Carolina. Minivans wind their way up the coast to Boston and down to D.C.

What a gift they gave us with their wedding. Letting us stop time for just a moment and ask ourselves:

"Hey. Was that us?"

CONNECTING TO ACTION

- What were the Aha Moments you found in the story? Did they remind you of any of your own?

- The stewardship in this story was reflected in the characters being part of a larger family, one that was larger than any individual or nationality. The ways that the family took care of each other. The genetic connections were not as important as the emotional bonds. When you think of your own important emotional bonds, what are the immediate Aha Moments that come to mind?

- The idea of "stopping time" is used in this story. If you could look back at your life and stop time, where would you stop it? That moment is an Aha Moment. What about that moment might lead you to work?

PART SEVEN:
SNAPSHOTS OF FINDING WORK

USING SNAPSHOTS OF SUCCESS

The stories in our first six chapters explored the Five Principles in depth. We saw the principles at work in a variety of settings, on a larger canvas that makes them real to us all.

We harnessed the power of the stories for one simple purpose: to prompt you to think differently about the way you search for work. To avoid generalized, clichéd solutions and find your own unique path.

In this next section, we narrow the focus. Instead of showing the Five Principles in the larger world, we turn to stories of a person successfully using one or more of our Five Principles to find work.

Thinking through these stories must be done with the same caution. You'll see that mimicking what these people do would never work for you. These stories show success, but they are unique to the individual at the center of each one. They are not meant to convey any message of "just do what this person did and you'll be fine."

Each of these snapshots shows a person putting an idea from the book into action in their own way. The people in these stories told their story, added music, communitized, solved mysteries, and practiced stewardship. They found work.

Which raises the central questions you'll want to consider as you read these stories: what's *your* way? How will you put the ways you now think differently about finding work into action?

SNAPSHOTS

What's in Your Wallet?

Jorge had worked steadily for 35 years, his entire adult life. A world-class mechanic, he could take a car engine apart with blinding speed. He'd never once taken a handout from anyone, never even thought about it, until the bad times hit early in 2008.

He'd launch into a story about the four guys he worked with at the garage. After about sixty seconds, you'd know the life story of these guys. Jorge, a natural storyteller, told the story so well that you felt like you'd known his subjects forever.

It was as if Jorge carried stories in his pocket, right next to his wallet. When it came time to pay his way, Jorge never faltered in pulling out the wallet. Any opening at all for a story? Jorge could reach in his pocket and pull one of those out, too.

He'd also spent years as a cook in downtown Chicago. "Oh yeah, the mayor?" Jorge would start out. "Nicest guy you ever met. He'd come in all the time …" and then off he'd go. Another story.

Jorge told stories, so people remembered him; they got to know him quickly.

That last job loss. That's what sent him to the social service agency—the absolute last place Jorge wanted to be. But for him, it had always been about family. His family needed medical care and help with housing. So he planted himself in that line for his family. That was the only way he could will himself to do it.

Funny thing about some storytellers. They can be the most private, even the shyest people in the world. Much more comfortable with just themselves and maybe a family member or friend. But the stories were so good, so constant, that no one ever realizes how private they want to be. Jorge was like that.

As he got to know the people who worked at the community center, he began to see that this place was different from what he had expected. The workers actually talked with the people in line for services. They shared stories as a way of getting through these hard times.

When it came to sharing stories, Jorge was a very rich man.

He'd take the help for his family. But he'd also become a volunteer. Jorge had never volunteered for anything in his life. He'd always been too busy working.

As the months went on, Jorge became a fixture in the place. His personal bond with the center grew. He had found a place where the lines between who needed help and who gave help just didn't matter. For Jorge, work at the center became second nature because he always had a story to share.

His stories were like gifts handed out to anyone who happened to be around.

Then one day a paid position opened up at the center. Of course Jorge got the job. He got it right away. He was already working at the place. Everyone knew there was no better choice.

Jorge had found work. Because everyone, literally everyone knew his story.

Working Out

Mike didn't just have an MBA. He had two of them. In finance and human resources, from one of the most prestigious schools in the country. Yes, it's rare. But it happens. The calls from Fortune 50 recruiters when he graduated were like yelping dogs clamoring for red meat.

Mike settled on a commercial real estate firm. He made his first million by the time he was 27, and then he bought, with his orthopedic surgeon wife, the summerhouse in Cabo.

But he was miserable. Commercial real estate just wasn't him. The thrill of the deal simply wasn't enough; he needed something that moved faster, so he decided to try trading. He bought a seat on the Chicago Stock

Exchange. He liked the speed, the risk, and the real danger of it all. It really was heart pounding.

Then he got into derivatives. Where he lost it all. Everything. The money, the houses, even the showpiece successful wife.

If he hadn't had the gym to help with the stress, the loss, the devastation of it all, he really didn't know what he would have done. Whereas he used to feel lucky if he made it there twice a week, now he was there every day. He loved it. Sometimes he'd be working out and drift off into worlds that made him forget all of it.

He was drifting one day when he heard his name being called. "Yo! Muscle dude! Mike!" He looked up from the bench where he was pressing two hundred pounds, and framed by the weight was Phil, the manager of the gym.

Phil spotted him as he glided the weight back into place and then stood up.

"Mike," Phil said. "Listen, you know Benito, tall guy, personal trainer? You know what a drama it is with him. Always something. Today he calls and says that a repo man was taking his car, there was an incident, and he can't come in this afternoon because he's in effen jail! Do you think you could take his clients this afternoon? He's got three coming in."

"I've never trained anybody in my life!"

"You got a routine for yourself, right?"

"Well, I start with that. Then I, ah ... improvise."

Mike did the afternoon. As 6:00 rolled around, he felt like he had come out from under some sort of blanket. Like he was seeing light for the first time. He loved being a personal trainer. *Loved* it.

On his way out, Phil stopped him and asked how it went. Before Mike could even begin to explain that in all his schooling, all his high-powered jobs, he had always felt like something was missing. He knew it was crazy. Personal trainers make no money. He *knew* that.

But in every other job he had felt like he was fooling himself, and in this one all that was gone. There was no self-deception here. He was Mike. A personal trainer. Nothing more to say.

Before he could even say any of that, Phil told him that the thing with Benito was a bit more serious than the car and the repo man. Turned out there were some details of the legal kind. Benito wouldn't be working at the gym anymore. So there was a need at that gym.

Before Phil could even ask him if he was interested in working as a personal fitness trainer, Mike said, "What would it take for me to get this job? I was born to do this work."

Who's to Blame?

Rick had been waiting for a decision on whether he'd get the job for four months. Megan was the hiring manager. Rick and Megan had connected on their very first phone conversation. They were laughing together within the first five minutes, and by the end of the conversation, it was as if they had known each other all their lives. Megan had national responsibility for the call centers of a for-profit college. Rick had run an operation the size of Megan's, but the job they were talking about was running just one center in Atlanta. Rick's hometown.

If it had only been Megan's decision, it would have been easy. Megan had figured out along the way that the strength of her organization depended on getting the best people. That sounds simple, but it's not. Especially in times when there are no jobs, people feel threatened—and the real goal is too often to hire someone who is controllable. Someone who *wouldn't* be a threat. So hiring a more experienced person took real self-assurance. The good news was that Megan had that self-assurance. She wanted the best. That's why she chose Rick.

But as the months dragged on, Rick saw that there was much more to the story. Specifically, the other twelve people, besides Megan, that he needed to impress to get the job. Each of these twelve people had real decision-making power. That was the way the organization worked.

The worst part? The one guy who ended up not liking Rick was the very last in the string of people. Only one of the twelve gave thumbs down. But that was enough.

When Megan called Rick to tell him that he didn't get the job, she was crestfallen. Rick ended up giving her an hour's worth of executive coaching on the hows and whys of an organization whose real goal is not results or productivity but is, in fact, control.

Within that hour of both Rick and Megan telling and sharing the story of why Rick was not hired, there was a moment when Rick said something that Megan never forgot. He said, "You really can't blame anyone for this. All you can do is tell the story as clearly as you can, without judging or blaming. Not because we're such good people, but because blaming doesn't help. We have to describe what happened so I can learn and you can make your shop a better place to work. But no one has to be blamed."

Both Rick and Megan made a valuable professional contact. Rick got better at spotting situations where work search was unfair. Megan learned how to tell the story of work search gone wrong without blaming anyone.

Two years later, when Rick (now a senior VP of customer service) needed a self-assured leader to run his eastern region, he immediately thought about Megan.

Rick gave her a call to catch up. They talked for an hour on the phone. Rick didn't even have to pay recruiting costs, read resumes, or go through an HR-driven process.

He simply hired Megan. He needed that self-assurance. The kind of person who thinks *business* before they think *blame*.

Megan was a perfect fit for the job.

MUSIC SET

Jack's Musical Note

Jack knew he didn't have a chance of getting this job. Not because he wouldn't be great at it. The obstacle was that he hadn't performed that job in several years. Jack knew that in the job search line, the question "How good are you at this job?" always mattered less than "How recently have you done the job?"

But he decided to send the resume anyway because that's all he knew how to do.

As he pressed the send key on his computer, he had the thought that if his resume were a piece of music, it would only have one note. Perhaps someone would read it. But probably not. There was really no way to know. Jack knew that this was the way the world worked when you were standing in the job search line.

The company Jack wanted to work for was brand-spanking new. Reinventing a whole market as it grew larger and more profitable by the hour. This was a company so innovative that the founder, Randy, was a prized guest on local news talk shows.

One night after watching Randy speak with a refreshing authenticity on the subject of resumes, an authenticity rarely seen in brand-new business leaders at the highest levels, Jack decided to take a different approach to seeking work at Randy's company. He decided to send in a resume that had more than one note.

Jack wrote Randy a letter that in effect invited Randy into his living room to continue the conversation Randy had started on television.

Everything about this note was unorthodox. It broke every rule on how to write a cover letter. It assumed a level of familiarity that would likely not occur between two people who had never met. It seemed too long.

In short, it was not a business letter. It was more like a piece of music with lots of notes. So it was a risk.

But what the letter did was paint the picture of an authentic conversation. So it left an impression that no other candidate even came close to leaving. The reader might not like the note. But he would not forget it.

The letter mirrored the kind of conversation Randy would have with Jack if they ever met in real life.

It told a sliver of Jack's story in a way that connected directly to Randy and his new company. Jack was picturing a duet as he wrote it. If the letter got to Randy, he could hate it. But he could also love it. Love it enough to bring Jack in for a real conversation. Even though there was that risk—because not everyone wants to sing in a duet.

Somehow HR did not stop the letter. Which was a mystery. The letter *did* get to Randy. Having never seen a letter like that, Randy, showing a trait very common among high-level leaders, simply got curious. So he had Jack in for a conversation and liked the fact that Jack was the same person on paper as he was in real life. Randy knew within five minutes that Jack could put his vision of customer service into the market. Two weeks later, Jack was working at Randy's company.

Jack's "musical" letter:

Dear Mr. Madison,

It was right after you said, "resumes are lies" on the "City TV Tonight" show that I said to my wife, "Oh crap. He's right."

"And that's the guy you really should be working for," she answered, pointing at you on TV. "Even though the chances of that are about the same as winning the Powerball lottery, because of course he is not going to read a resume. That's a guy who *wants* smart people, like you, around him. Not people who write resumes."

"I'm sure my resume has already been tossed. Randy obviously knows that blathering on about how great you were at the last job means nothing. Plus, unsolicited e-mails tossed over the virtual transom," I said to my wife, "don't usually get someone to respond. The guy probably won't write back."

"Well," she said, "they responded when you oversaw customer service and training for Sunshine Tea Stores. That all came from you writing a letter.

They didn't know you then. All they knew was that you could be really clear about what it took to keep a customer."

That was true, even if it was my wife speaking. So I thought I'd take a shot and say that if you did decide we'd have a real face-to-face conversation, I'd be ready to start the conversation with:

- A new way to think about your customer service. I coauthored a book on how to find the place where systems thinking meets customer service.

- Cutting your turnover costs in half.

- Measuring what matters.

- Creating a defined path from talent to stock increase.

- Making customer service a revenue stream.

- Finding and keeping the best people.

- Being the person you don't now have at the company. The coach who relates to everyone "gets" results and why we're here, and requires the absolute minimum of management time.

- Making your job more fun.

All of that, I've done. But the real point is how I could help do it at your company. How I could help you hang on to your customers.

So if you want to have that conversation, I could be there in about five minutes.

Take care,

Jack

The Work Whistle

In the mornings in Albuquerque just as the sun begins to rise, there is an orange glow that bathes the proud adobe heart of the small homes where Ramon has spent his whole life working hard. That orange morning light was like a daily prayer to Ramon. A voice that said, "Something good really could happen today. So I will do the only thing I know for sure. I will work as hard as I can."

The voice, to Ramon, was like music. Ramon liked all music. Salsa to classical. country to jazz. Sinatra to hip-hop. His friends and family laughed at the range of his musical tastes. But Ramon would simply shrug and say, "I always have a song in my head." Then he'd start whistling something no one had ever heard before.

Ramon was 52 years old. The jobs he'd had? He couldn't even remember all of them, but the constant thread in all was that he had worked as hard as he could.

But as there were no full-time jobs to be found right now, Ramon decided that he'd try day labor.

He knew the corner where the man came with the truck to pick up the workers. Everyone knew that corner. He knew that for every ten working men who would gather and wait, the man in the truck might point at four, motion them to the back of the truck, and drive away. He knew the work could be anything. Passing out flyers on the other side of town, picking up litter downtown, hauling garbage. He knew that at the end of the day there was no guarantee he'd get paid. But this was all there was right now. The important thing, the most important thing, the only thing was that when the man in the truck drove up, he would point at you.

So one Wednesday morning, when Ramon walked into the orange glowing light just before sunrise, there was a warm breeze blowing in from the desert just as the truck rolled up. Twenty men standing on the corner. Maybe eight of them would get work.

All twenty men stood quietly as the man climbed down out of the driver's seat whistling the first two lines of an old song about a summer wind.

Just as the man put his foot on the ground and scanned the quiet crowd, whistling two lines of that familiar song about the wind in summer, Ramon, without even thinking, finished the next two lines of the song, whistling the song with words he didn't know but a melody he knew as well as his name.

The man looked over at Ramon. A light went on in the man's eyes as he pointed at Ramon and motioned him up to the back of the truck for a day of work.

The man pointed at seven more men and then climbed into the cab, and as the truck started down the road into the rising orange sun, the man said to the driver: "How 'bout that. Guy knew Sinatra. He knew my song."

Banging on Drums

Sam had a talent that he had never explained to anyone. They'd think he was crazy. Sam's talent was his ability to make management clichés *mean* something.

Imagine hearing "the customer is always right" (a phrase that others call "retail's biggest lie") and translating that phrase into some sort of action.

Sam first discovered he had that talent when he worked for Andy. Andy had a phrase that he would say over and over and over again.

> Authority, responsibility, accountability.

> Authority, responsibility, accountability.

Andy used the words constantly and drummed them into Sam's head— *drum* being the key word. Sam would imagine the words as a drumbeat. Silly as it sounded, that's what be did. Because when the words became like a drumbeat, it made Sam better able to make the words mean something in real life. Over the years, it got to the point where all Andy had to do is say Sam's name.

Then Sam could finish the take it from there, banging the drum himself.

> Authority, responsibility, accountability.

> Authority, responsibility, accountability.

It was that drumbeat that taught the words. When I say *taught* the words, I don't mean *define* them. That's the easy part. Teaching the words here meant guiding Sam to use the words in a way that made them mean something, make something happen, fix something, sell something, train someone, give someone an opportunity. That's the kind of teaching that takes hold.

Authority came first because it has power. You want to jump in a car and go visit a customer at 6:00 on a Friday night because something needs to be fixed? You have the authority to do that. You want to spend $100 to resolve a customer complaint because $10,000 of business was at stake? You have the power to do that.

Responsibility meant that you had to make sure it happened. You. Personally. You had to make sure that the $10,000 in business at stake actually came in the door.

Accountability meant that at the end of the day, if the $10,000 wasn't in the company's bank account, then you had to have an explanation as to why not. Answer and then fix the problem. If it was in the bank account, then all credit went to you.

The words had meaning. Like the sound of the drum.

Which is why one Monday morning in the tomato sauce aisle of the grocery store, after accidently bumping Andy's cart, Sam looked up out of his perpetual haze, saw Andy, whom he hadn't seen in years, and instead of saying "Whoops" or "Sorry" or "How've you been?" Sam looked at Andy and said, "Authority, responsibility, accountability."

That bass drum was still playing.

Andy laughed and said, "That's right!"

The two pulled their grocery carts over to the side and caught up. It didn't take long. Andy was spending his last Monday morning grocery shopping. The following week he was taking over as CEO of a new company, and of course he wanted Sam to sign up to run operations.

They agreed to talk later in the week. As Sam stood waiting in the checkout line, the notes of that bass drum started up again.

Authority, responsibility, accountability.

Authority, responsibility, accountability.

A repeating rhythm that would make this new company successful, too.

Let Someone Else Sing Your Song

Kristen was a teacher. She had always been a teacher. It's all she knew how to do.

She had started out teaching high school. Then special education for emotionally disturbed kids. From there, she discovered that what she was really good at was being a coach. As she got better, she realized that she excelled at coaching adults.

She went into "corporate training," "talent management"—all sorts of different names that came down to the same thing: helping someone else get better at what they do. That was it.

To her, work was like a chorus. Singing together just sounded better. When she was teaching teachers and managers, or writing the training, or delivering the work, planning, or training sessions herself, it became like a chorus. She loved every minute of it.

Until the time when there were no jobs. Teachers were being laid off in every city. If you worked with adults in business to help them reach their goals? That was now like being a blacksmith.

So Kristen got in the job search line. It made her very tired, very fast. She knew the goal was to sell herself. She'd done sales training that had generated millions and millions of dollars for the folks she supported. She'd even sold her training. But selling herself was different.

It was as if she was trying to sing every part in the chorus herself. It just wasn't working.

So she started thinking. She had spent her life helping others be better singers. Why stop now? So Kristen decided that she'd be quiet.

Perhaps the wisest move by anyone in a helping profession.

She decided she'd be quiet and let the other members of the chorus sing her praises.

Kristen wrote a letter. She used others' words. It was as if she was putting together her own chorus. She used variations of the letter for 50 organizations where there might be work. She showed them, through the letter, that no one had to teach her how to be harmonious. It's just the way she was. By adding the harmony she showed in the chorus of quotes from others, she had three new offers for work two months later.

Adding harmony got Kristen work.

Now Kristen gets to sing in a chorus where everyone is on key, singing the very same song.

Kristen's letter:

Dear Ms. White,

Speaking directly to your three criteria for the program manager role, I thought I'd share the words of others on what kind of a fit I'd be.

Collaboration: Beth Ohura. Director of Professional Development, Chicago Public Schools

I've known Kristen Sang for a number of years; she has a success record for building leadership capacity for the full spectrum of educators all over the world. In my role as Chicago Public Schools Director of Principal Professional Development, and later as a CPS principal, I saw Kristen demonstrate a commitment to the children of Chicago above and beyond. Having been in both the private and public sectors, she brings a unique set of talents. As a staff developer, Kristen puts others first. She is enthusiastic and articulate, and sensitive to the people with whom she is working. She has an amazing ability to strategize, so her methods match the learning needs and styles of the people in front of her. I strongly urge you to consider her for a position.

Curriculum Development and Delivery: Robert Alexander. Vice President, Southern Data

Kristen invigorated our leadership development program at Southern Data. She is a thoughtful leader who knows how to implement. She developed programs that were known for pertinent content that challenged status-quo thinking. These programs allowed senior leaders to evaluate current leadership skills and to embrace new skills. Her in-depth knowledge of this practice area gave her a tremendous amount of credibility with the leaders at Southern Data. Her leadership of professional development brought a sense of harmony to the team. I would recommend Kristen to any organization looking to increase their leadership skills.

Delivering the Training: Melissa Waller. Vice President, Telecom, Inc.

I was privileged enough to have Kristen as an instructor/trainer for a year-long leadership candidate program I was involved in at Telecom. Upon initially meeting Kristen, I was immediately drawn to her charisma and approachability. She is one of the best motivators I have ever been around; she is a very positive and creative thinker who has a very real talent for putting context around anything that comes up in discussions. Her knowledge and ability to "link the world together" are a very rare combination. She always promoted an atmosphere of true and honest knowledge sharing among the group involved and never made you feel like any comment was unwelcome. She genuinely cares about others, and I loved to witness her in action. I was in awe of her every day. I've never met anyone who is more inspiring and who promotes the growth and development of others like Kristen does.

As you review the mountain of resumes composed of folks talking about themselves, my hope is that you'll remember this note, composed of other people talking about what I could bring to your company.

It would be a true joy if this prompted a conversation with you.

Take care,

Kristen Sang

Tea Party

A Christmas Eve snow swept down and muffled the raw energy of the Chicago Loop only a little. Cars and voices and the rivers of people rushing through the streets and the stores, a deep-voiced Santa Claus ringing a golden bell and singing holiday songs at the corner of State and Randolph Streets.

Josef, with all the holiday jobs long since filled, was heading home, past a tea shop. There stood a scared-looking young lady. Hunched quietly over tray of samples. Her tiny hot cups of sweet black tea, steaming and then getting cold fast.

Josef's heart went out to the young lady who simply didn't know what to do. Josef had worked the tea and coffee shops back in Warsaw. He knew the business well. He knew that this kind of sampling would never get anyone into the store.

So as he stopped for a sample, he smiled and said to the young lady, "Well, why don't you sing?"

"Excuse me?"

"We will find a song! It is easy! I will help you."

Josef began to sing a totally made up song in a booming loud voice even louder than the Santa Claus bells clamoring on the corner.

Jingle bell friend sings

Have some tea

Good for you and me!

The young lady started laughing. Josef repeated the verse just as the owner of the teashop came out the door, passing someone who had sampled the tea and was now walking in. Josef was having so much fun, he forgot for a moment that he was in Chicago. For just one tiny moment, he imagined himself back in Warsaw. When he saw the owner come out of the shop and stare at him, Joseph said, "Good evening, sir," in Polish.

The owner's smile lit up the city night, as he answered back in Polish, "Good evening to you sir! I believe you somehow know the song of our store. I believe your song can sell our tea. May I speak to you for a moment?"

Josef went inside the store. It was warmer there. The two began to talk. That conversation turned out to be Josef's job interview.

Josef had a wonderful Christmas that year. Because he knew that the next day he'd be at work, singing all the passing people into the warmth of the tea store.

COMMUNITIZED

The Other Web

A middle-aged couple sat in their living room on a Sunday afternoon. She has just lost her job.

"It's funny," she said. "Every time I think about that time, when the business was first starting, this song goes through my head."

"Umm," he answered. Eyes glued to the football game on TV.

"Not sure what it was called. Something like 'Peace and the River.' You remember that song?"

"Not really."

"It was awhile ago. Everything was so crazy at the plant back then. Everybody said manufacturing done by little shops, customized orders, big customer service, all of that was dead. You had to be big. That was it. No one knew what was going on. The line would stop three times a shift. Everybody had to be moved around. No one even knew I wasn't a supervisor. If anybody asked I'd say, 'I just play a supervisor on TV.' Place was crazy. Then the bosses started in with six sigma programs. I read the books at night. I remember one of them talking about me and saying, 'we're gonna be making her a supervisor. So why don't we just do it now?' That's how I got to be a supervisor. I never really had a job interview. I just started doing the job. You sure you don't remember that song?"

"I don't even remember why the Bears are a pro team."

"I wish I could remember the words to that song. I can hear the tune in my head. The words were all about plans changing, people going way

174

too fast in every direction. Every time I hear that tune though, I think of those days when work was crazy busy, but it was good. It was like the tune told the story of the place."

"Yeah," he said. "I wish everything was crazy good now. I wish every place was like the Ford plant on Torrence Avenue adding those jobs. I bet that's going to be crazy. Probably have six, seven thousand people standing in line for the jobs. Too bad we don't know anybody in human resources."

"We know Betty," she said.

"Betty's in quality control."

"Close enough," she said, "but she's also next door. You don't mind if I slip across the driveway to borrow a cup of sugar, do you?"

"Go ahead!"

Betty was sitting at her kitchen table alone, drinking a cup of coffee, the sounds of the football game coming from the next room. She smiled when she heard the knock on the back door, and thought, "Yeah! Someone to talk to!"

Betty told her she was ecstatic about the revival of the plant. Even if it was just a tiny start. Her friend Irma in human resources had a tough job ahead of her. They needed real top-notch supervisors for the line before they did anything. Irma just didn't have time to wade through the applications of the three thousand people who'd be lining up for work.

The woman from next door smiled and said, "Well, maybe I can help with that. Do you want to put me in contact with Irma?"

Two weeks later, the woman from across the driveway was a supervisor at the new plant.

What got her the job? It was the way she spoke in the interview about keeping the business going when things got crazy. She talked about the crazy times at work, and the ways she'd be able to calm everybody down and get everybody back to work. In fact, the way she talked about calming people down, it was almost like she was singing a song.

Crossing the Street

Tommy read in a newspaper one morning that he was "underemployed." He'd never heard the word before. For all he knew, there was no such word until the jobs started disappearing. "Underemployed" could mean all the doctors and lawyers working at Starbucks. But for Tommy, what it meant was that his one job no longer paid the bills.

Tommy still had his job. Day bartender in a place that served lunch near the ballpark. He'd worked most of the bars in the neighborhood for most of his life. Even been part owner of one once.

The bars were kind of like a neighborhood inside a neighborhood. Everybody who worked the bars knew each other. Even if it was only to offer a nod in passing at the end of a long, hard Friday night. It was a community.

But business was down everywhere. That meant tips were down. Tommy couldn't make it on what he earned anymore. He had to do something else and do it quick.

Tommy was a big, friendly guy with a winning smile who knew how to handle a drunk. That was it. So if there were no more jobs as bartenders and the job he had wasn't cutting it, then Tommy was in trouble. They could call it "underemployed" in the papers. He called it trouble.

As Tommy leafed through this book, he saw the article on the soldier. "Communitizing Safety." He liked that one. Tommy had been in Vietnam, something he didn't talk about. He liked the article about the soldier. He understood what the author was talking about when he talked about "keeping us safe."

But the army was ancient history. Another life; it couldn't help him find a bartending job. He could stare down the wildest raving maniac on the street. Tommy had a presence that just made wild eyed drunks get sober real fast. Tommy would shoot a look, and the problem was solved. But he was no soldier. Not anymore. So he put this book down and forgot about it. He had too much on his mind to worry about not being a soldier anymore. He needed a job.

But he remembered the phrase "keeping us safe." For some reason, it stuck in his head.

A week or so later, he was on his way home at 6:00 when he saw Gino, the guy who handled security at the bar across the street. The two men stopped for a minute to catch up. Gino said to Tommy, "Hey, I guess this is it. I just gave my notice. Going back to Baltimore to look after my Ma. She's getting on."

"You're a good son, Gino," Tommy said, "but we'll all be sorry to see you go!"

"Yeah, I guess that keeping the bar safe will be somebody else's gig," said Gino.

That, of course, turned the light bulb on above Tommy's head. "Hey Gino, I've been looking for something else, pulling a double shift. You think they'd bring me on there to do security?"

"You kidding? Of course! Let's go get it done right now."

Five minutes later, Tommy was no longer underemployed. He was working at a job across the street that had never even been advertised.

He was "keeping us safe."

Marketing Strategy

Cassandra had been looking for a job for six months. She had a great resume. She practiced her interviewing skills. Talked about how she loved people and always gave an example. But of course, as she heard every day, everywhere she turned, there were no jobs.

So it was a real shock to find that when she started thinking about finding *work* instead of a *job*, it took her all of an hour to be successful.

It was at the Farmer's Market. In Boston, farmers would haul their produce and baked goods into the city every Saturday morning. Cassandra would always go early. Once, she was there so early that a woman unloading home-baked pies hadn't finished setting up. So Cassandra just naturally started helping. She and the woman started talking, and something just clicked. In fifteen minutes they pretty much knew each other's life stories. As the customers started coming, Cassandra stuck around and just naturally fell into helping. After forty-five minutes it became clear to Cassandra that her new friend was very, very bad with math. At first she didn't say anything, but when the woman began to mistakenly give away $10.00 in change, Cassandra couldn't help herself. She jumped in. That led to a conversation on bookkeeping. Turns out that the woman basically didn't do any. It was a good day if she had a fat roll of singles in her pocket,

Cassandra started talking, and after fifteen minutes, the woman said to her, "Gee, do you think maybe I could pay you to do my books?"

At the sixty-minute mark, Cassandra had work. As she walked home, her bag stuffed with vegetables and a cherry pie, she had the thought, "There are twenty-five other stands at that market. What if ten of them needed someone to do their books?"

No Lights, No Camera, Just Action

Terri had worked customer service jobs ever since she came back to Gulfport to help her Mom after Katrina hit. She had made sure her Mom was back on her feet. Then came the recession.

They got through that because the casinos were still strong.

But then came the oil spill. It seemed like everything all around her started falling downhill at once. First, her Mom's health, which she couldn't do much about because of preexisting conditions, then Terri was laid off, then she started coughing. Didn't know why, and couldn't afford to find out.

Terri was an Oprah fan. If she knew Oprah, she thought, she wouldn't have any of these problems at all.

That prompted the thought, "I wonder if it would be harder to get Oprah or the people at Pete's Payroll Services to talk to me?"

She knew the answer. Probably Oprah—but maybe not. Pete had the last open customer service job in town. Getting through to anyone at Pete's was hard enough. Actually talking to somebody at Pete's Payroll? It was kind of like ... well, she thought, it really was like talking to a celebrity.

She had just finished reading Oprah's biography. The book made her feel like in some way, she knew Oprah. And then came the "epiphany." That sudden idea that seemed to appear out of nowhere. "If I can know Oprah, maybe I can know the people at Pete's. What if I did a little research on the people at Pete's? What if I could figure out something I had in common with them? Everybody else would be talking about how qualified they were for that job, and I'd be talking about what I had in common with the people making the hiring decision!"

So Terri did a little detective work, and then she wrote this quick note. She used the real names of the people who ran Pete's. She showed what she had in common with Pete's and its customer base. The note got her in to talk to the folks at Pete's Payroll Services. It was different than the other hundred letters they received about the job. It wasn't just a resume. This note was personal, like a song written just for the good folks at Pete's.

When Pete saw that Terri wasn't just qualified, but she was one of them—really part of their community—Terri found work.

Terri's quick note:

Dear Pete's Payroll Service,

My fit as your Customer Service Manager looks exceptionally strong:

- Like Ms. Silver: I've managed customer service groups of five to ten people.

- Like Mr. Gunther: I've worked with some of the world's best sales teams. One team went from zero to 75 percent market share against a division of ABC Payroll.

- Like Pete's customer base: I have been a small business owner.

- Like all Pete's Payroll employees: I know the rewards of a fast-paced, high-energy company where people line up at the door to work alongside of you, in both good and bad economic times.

When we have a face-to-face conversation, I'll be able to close any gaps you might see between my resume and your job specs. Then we can get on to the exciting part, which is not what I've done, but rather how I can immediately help your team make a great company even better.

Let's talk soon!

Terri Ann Gibson

Greetings

Noel did not need the job. No matter what it paid or didn't pay. He didn't even need to work at all, much less two jobs. Not at age 84.

He had always worked. Since leaving the Royal Air Force as a young man, he had built a successful practice as an architect. He was still an architect. Still working. That never went away. Perhaps "semiretired," but certainly not retired. He lived in a small green mountain village in Wales.

In his younger years, there were at least five local pubs in the area, perhaps more. But now, with the changes in the business and the global recession, there was only one. Noel would stop in two or three times a week, always on the same days.

Noel always liked to support the locals, of course—especially in hard times. He would take his seat at the bar, near the front door. He knew everyone. He knew the owner well, a hard man. He was roughened and left cynical by all his years behind the bar, and that didn't make him any more friendly with the customers, either. Noel knew how close the owner was to shutting down. But there was one thing Noel didn't know.

Noel didn't know that every time he was in the pub, business went up. Sometimes as high as 10 %.

The owner didn't know why Noel brought in business, but he knew what his books were telling him. On the nights Noel was in the pub, business improved. So he decided he'd pay more attention to the twinkly-eyed older gentleman and find out his secret.

It didn't take long. As the owner watched Noel hold forth from his seat at the bar, he realized that first and foremost, Noel almost never forgot a name. When he did forget, he asked, and then used the person's name.

He ended up addressing everyone by name. It seemed like such a small thing—there had to be more.

As he kept his eye on Noel, he realized that Noel was doing something else. Again, it was so small; one could miss it if one were not careful. Noel was welcoming everyone who walked in the place. Everyone! Even when the owner might have waved or said hello to a patron, Noel would burst out with, "In case no one has told you yet, let me be the first to welcome you!"

Could that be it? Calling a person by name and then authentically welcoming them? That was all it took?

After a week of this, the owner was looking at his books one night and realized it was true. Noel was increasing business in the pub! Astounding.

From that day on, Noel never paid for another drink—something that of course bothered him, at first. "What's the occasion?" he'd ask. At first the owner would just smile and say, "We're glad you're here, Noel." But after one or two quizzical looks, the owner broke down and spilled the secret. "Noel, when you're here, I do better business."

"Ah," said Noel. "I am all for better business! I suppose we could do this. Just as long as the work never became a job!"

"Of course, of course," said the owner. "All you have to do is be you."

"Well, that happens to be my specialty," smiled Noel as he raised his glass.

As he did, some old friends came in the door. "Ah, Marnie and Keith! Gloria! Hello David and Shannon! Welcome! Cold outside, eh? Come in!"

Protect and Serve

Tom found work soon after his girlfriend Ann had the gun stuck in her face by a New York City police officer. Ann had been counting out the change at the register of the bookstore one morning. He had just gone across the street to get coffee; as he was walking back, he saw the cop calmly walk into the store, gun drawn, and say to Ann, "Freeze. Your alarm just went off."

Tom heard Ann, who had nerves of steel, calmly answer, "Officer, we don't have an alarm."

"Is this 2907 Broadway?" asked the cop.

"No, this is 2807 Broadway," Ann answered.

"Oh. Well, excuse me then," said the cop, walking head down out the door right past Ann.

An hour later, when the owner came in, Ann told him the story. Then Tom started asking questions about the operational procedures in the store. Where were they written? How were people trained? How did the store guard against theft? On and on. Tom always asked a lot of questions.

Ann liked to read. Tom liked to ask questions.

As they were talking, the owner said to Tom, "Hey, how much would it cost me to have you write up an operational manual for me and train people in it?"

They talked a little more, and by lunchtime, Tom had found work. On the back of an old invoice, he drew out a plan for writing the manual and training the employees. He started doing the work the very next day.

Risk Rewards

Truth be told, Rick had always been a writer, but he had never really written anything. It sounded like a contradiction, but it wasn't. Rick supposed there were probably more than a few writers out there who felt the same way. I'm a writer, but witty letters to my friends do not exactly constitute a body of work.

So when the real writer, the published writer, one of the company's "cash cows" sent his new manuscript around the office asking for feedback, Rick was being more than a little presumptuous when he did a total rewrite of chapter eight.

This was a family company. As political a culture as one could imagine. By doing a rewrite, Rick had just violated pretty much every political rule of the place. As a political player, Rick had the sophistication of a gnat.

But the real writer actually liked Rick's work. So did a few other folks. Before he knew it, the contract ghostwriter was gone, and Rick, who had accepted the challenge of the rewrite pretty much out of his own ignorance, was now the co-author of a real book.

Rick had finally found work as a writer.

MYSTERIES SOLVED

Reanimation

If there were an academic degree in the mystery of bringing something back to life, Linda would not need it.

She was born that way. No one ever had to teach her.

Linda's talent was to restore. At first glance, you might think she was simply fixing something, but it was more than that. She restored people, products, and places. Imagine a refrigerator breaking down; Linda wouldn't just repair the motor and get it working. She would go on and fill it with food that everyone would want. How did she know which food to fill it with? A mystery.

Her talent for breathing life into whatever needed restoring tripled her salary when she worked for a start-up software company. Look at her and you'd see the discipline, the follow-up, a gargantuan work ethic, and the fact that she took personal responsibility for everything she did. But spend a few hours with her and you'd see that mysterious ability to restore in action, in both small and large ways. Some people called her the heart and soul of the company.

From corporate project management, the next phase of her journey landed her smack in the middle of a group of tiny children's dreams.

She became a ballet teacher, specializing in tiny ballerinas as young as 18 months old. Again, Linda restored—breathing life into the program. Linda transferred love of dance and creative movement to hundreds of tiny ballerinas through the years.

Linda found that her real love was the inevitable tiny little girl in the pink tutu who stood on the side of the room, the oddball kid who didn't seem to fit in, the quiet kid, the scared kid. Miss Linda became a celebrity to her little students when they'd see her in the streets and grocery stores of the town. How did she solve the mystery of the tiny kid who stood apart from the crowd? That tiny kid that was always unique? It was a mystery. Miss Linda got kids started on loving dance. Got them started on something that many would carry with them all their lives.

It was in one of those grocery store conversations with a parent—as a little ballerina peeked up shyly to gaze in awe at Miss Linda—that led her to the mysterious transition of finding work in cupcakes and cookies.

In that grocery store, Miss Linda and the parent, who happened to own a number of coffeehouses, were talking over the bread display about how hard it was to find good pastry. That led to declining pastry sales in the coffee shop business. Miss Linda said that maybe she could help. The parent said she'd take all the help she could get.

So three days later, Miss Linda dropped by the coffeehouse not with a resume but with a loaf or her homemade olive bread. When the olive bread sold out in seven minutes, Miss Linda never again needed a resume.

The olive bread became a regular item at the five-store chain. Six months later, just by chance, an executive chef with a worldwide following dropped by one of the stores and tried a piece. The executive chef knew her business, so she knew she had to track down Linda. The olive bread was a valuable product.

Elizabeth, the executive chef, made a few calls and found, again just by coincidence, that Miss Linda was an old friend of her brother's. The mysteries of a small world.

Elizabeth and Linda met for lunch. Within a week, the chef was calling Linda to problem solve at restaurants that needed help. First around the city, then the country. Whenever something in a menu needed to have new life breathed into it, Elizabeth sent Linda. People in the business came to know that when Elizabeth said, "I'll send Linda. She'll know what to do," they had just received a promise that would go straight to their bottom line.

Elizabeth's consulting practice grew at a steady 15 % year after year and is still growing today.

Never once did Linda write a resume. Once when another national company had heard about Linda's work history and called her with a job offer, the HR director asked her to send a resume. Linda laughed and said, "I suppose I can make one. Except the one thing I can't figure out is how do I get the taste of my olive bread on the resume?"

Hidden Talents

When the administrator of the nature museum said to Bethany, "If you ever want to work here, please send me a resume," Bethany gave her an embarrassed smile and said, "Gosh, I don't even have a resume."

The administrator answered, "Well, call me. Or something. Because I've never seen somebody do what you just did."

"It was really nothing," Bethany answered. "I have lots of nieces and nephews. I've been around kids a lot. But thank you."

"No, thank *you*," said the administrator. "We could have had a real scene in here, and you controlled it."

What had just happened in the airy, glass-enclosed tropical jungle of the museum's butterfly garden wasn't all that complicated. A young teacher, just out of her master's in education program and in her first week on the job, had been leading a field trip of squirming, energetic four-year-olds through the butterfly garden. One of the larger butterflies had landed on the head of one little boy, who began to panic and shout, "The butterfly is gonna eat me!" His panic spread like gasoline on a fire, and within five seconds all fifteen of the tiny kids were screaming, the young teacher was shocked into silence and losing control of the group, and the screams of the kids were echoing off the glass walls of the butterfly garden room like sirens.

Seeing the young teacher paralyzed into silence, Bethany, who had been on the garden path right behind the group of kids, called out, "Hey kids, look at me!"

The authority in her voice immediately drew fifteen pairs of children's eyes. As the screaming stopped, the children grew curious and watched as Bethany held out her right hand, palm up, and said, "Now see what happens."

As if on cue, a butterfly landed on her palm. "See?" she said. "The butterfly is your friend! He won't hurt you!"

The incident was over as quickly as it had begun.

Bethany forgot about it all, until six months later when all the jobs, including hers, went away. She was searching the Web when she saw a job listed at the nature museum. The job listed an advanced degree as a preference. Bethany had graduated only from high school. She would never get a job like that. Putting herself up as a candidate, she worried, would be dishonest. Maybe even just a little bit like lying.

Still the administrator had given her a business card...

So she used it. The administrator remembered her right away, invited her in, and they talked for two hours.

The educational qualifications never came up. They didn't need to. They were irrelevant. Just like Bethany's concerns about being honest.

Bethany had devoured the information on the museum's Web site. She'd also been a visitor dozens of times. Her natural ability to make nature exciting for kids came through in everything she said. The administrator had decided to hire her within the first five seconds of the conversation.

History's Mystery

In the tightly knit world of the auto body business in Los Angeles, they called Ron "Professor Painter." Everybody knew him and respected his skill in the paint booth. They gave him grief about always lecturing somebody on something. Telling stories. Bringing up some obscure fact. When the TV show *Cheers* was at its height, Ron was often compared to the know-it-all mailman, Cliff Clavin.

Truth be told, Ron was just curious. About pretty much everything. His amazing skill as a paint man in the shops had allowed him to make a comfortable living his whole life. He was born to do flawless work. He did it in L.A., where the standards were very, very high. But the other advantage of his trade was it allowed long hours of pure thinking time. In the paint booth, Ron's skill took over while his head circled the universe of all the literature he'd read late at night when no one was around, all the music he'd heard, all the art he'd seen. Ron had finished high school long ago. Then he really started learning.

The results of this massive input of fact, fiction, and imagination were stories. Some he kept to himself. When he could get someone to listen, he shared them. Every now and then, he'd even write one and post it somewhere on the Internet.

But he also used his stories to help work out whatever mystery or challenge he was facing. Sometimes he found that if he could just make up a story about a problem, the story itself would bring the solution.

Ron's immediate problem was that that autobody shops were shutting their doors faster than a tricked-out 1962 cherry red Corvette roaring down a desert road when no one was watching. Even a top-tier paint man like Ron couldn't find work. He'd spent his days going from shop to shop. Ron was a paint man, and he was thorough. So he hit every shop. Of course he asked for a full-time job. That's all he'd ever known. He asked, but no one said yes.

Professor Painter was starting to believe that it was true, that there were no jobs. He had spent his whole life being a hopeful person. But slowly, as more and more people said no, fear was beating back hope.

Ron had more and more time on his hands, so he decided to make the whole situation into a story.

The premise of his new story, he thought as he drove on to the next auto body shop, would be this: What if three of history's great artists went looking for a job?

Ron had spent some time working for a corporation when he was younger; he knew a bit about how corporations worked. So Ron had his three artists looking for jobs in corporations.

As the story unfolded in his head, Ron wondered, "If I can figure out who among these three people in my story gets work first, maybe I can figure out how I could find work?"

So one Tuesday morning, driving from one shop to the next, Ron began to say his story out loud. Here's what Ron said as he drove the Los Angeles freeway system, going from body shop to body shop, looking for a full-time job. Ron called his story "Picasso, Joplin, and Kafka Interview for a Job."

An aging artist named Picasso opens the door that says "Human Resources," and peeks into the office. From behind the desk, a young woman of perhaps 23 stands up and motions him to sit.

"Thanks for coming in, Mr. Picasso. My name is Kristie. Any trouble finding the place?"

Picasso shrugs.

"Alrighty then. I'm going to be asking you a few questions about your background and experience. Then it will be your turn to ask me questions on this new role we've just put in place here at United Informers Equity. Then we can talk about next steps. Okey doke?"

Picasso shrugs.

"So, I understand you are some sort of an artist? Do I have that right?"

Picasso reaches for a piece of paper on her desk. Turns it over and quickly sketches a dove. Pushes it over the desk to Kristie. He has yet to say a word.

"I see." Kristie stands up and says, "Well, as you can imagine, we have lots and lots of people applying for this job. So we'll be in touch. I don't think we need to take any more of your time. Can you find your way out? Okay then. Have a great day."

Picasso shrugs and leaves the room.

One door down, in the next human resources office, a young singer named Janis Joplin knocks, and a younger man named Timmy, who is also Kristie's special friend at work, says, "Why, yes, Ms. Joplin. Thanks for coming in. Any trouble finding the place?"

Janis Joplin coughs. Clears her throat and says, "Got any coffee? Rough night last night."

Timmy frowns, cocks his head, and says, "I am so sorry, fresh out. But if I may? I understand you are some sort of singer? Is that right? Do you have a resume?"

Janis Joplin shakes her head no. Then says, "All I brought is this." She reaches over, runs her hand along the top of Timmy's monitor, and a video of her singing the song "Try (Just a Little Bit Harder)" begins to play.

"Well," says Timmy when the video ends. "That certainly was something. We will certainly let you know if anything comes up. These are hard times, you know, Ms. Joplin. So we'll let you know."

Finally, in an office way down at the end of the hall, a stoop-shouldered brooding young man with a very, very old soul named Franz Kafka coughs as he sits down.

The door of this office reads "The Worker's Accident Insurance Institute for the Kingdom of Bohemia."

"Ah, Herr Kafka," says Human Resources Director Betz. "So glad you could come in. It says here you are a writer?"

Kafka replies by quoting the first line of his book, "The Metamorphosis."

A story about a man who wakes up one morning and finds he has, to say the least, changed.

Director Betz slaps his palm on the polished oak top of his desk and says, "Splendid, Herr Kafka! You know that just this morning, we had a man go missing. A writer. Who knew we'd need another one! Herr Kafka? You're hired!"

Suddenly Ron felt his story was at an end. He laughed to himself, remembering how he always loved Kafka.

Then Ron started thinking, "How come Kafka found work? Why didn't Janis Joplin or Picasso?"

That was when it hit him. It was so simple that the Professor never saw it. Not until he started playing, making up stories.

Kafka was replacing a missing person. He arrived at just the right time. He was filling a need. Not just a job. A need. That's why he was the only one of the three artists who found work.

Ron was going from shop to shop because he knew people in each shop. But mostly because he was methodical. Liked to do things in an organized, logical, thorough manner. He was talking about his experience. Asking for the full time job. Even before he found out if the shop had any missing persons. *He was telling people what he had before finding out what they needed!*

Ron skipped the next shop. Pulled over into the parking lot of a Carl's Jr. hamburger joint. Started punching numbers on his cell phone. In an hour, he had contacted 10 shops—something that would have taken him a day if he had gone to all 10 in person. One of the shops, a nice operation run by an old friend named Lori who used to train shop owners in East L.A. back when they both had corporate jobs, was in panic mode.

Lori's painter had just stormed out. She had five vehicles to get out right now. She had a need.

Ron told her not to panic. Fifteen minutes later he was at her shop. Instead of trolling for jobs, Ron had work.

The Ginny Puzzle

Nobody operated the espresso machine worse than Ginny. It was a mystery how she could be so terrible at something so many others found easy. She simply couldn't do it. They even had a regional training manager, Barry, come in from Seattle. He spent 3 hours with Ginny. Barry was a guy who had an attention span of about thirty seconds—he drank a *lot* of coffee. But Ginny mystified him. How could somebody be that bad? She'd forget every measurement, reverse the procedures, forget the milk temperature, wash the thermometer with the counter rag. If a health inspector came in, they would have been shut down faster than you could order most drinks.

Perhaps it was a memory problem? The inability to follow directions? Or do the math? But it was getting to the point where *why* didn't matter. Barry had to let her go.

He directed Ginny to a table at a far corner of the café. There were no customers at that moment.

As they walked to that table a very strange thing happened.

Making their way through the store, Ginny would face, arrange, and straighten every single food item and every single piece of merchandise in the store. As she did so, Barry looked at her face. It was almost as if, relieved of the pressure of the machine, she slipped into some sort of trance that allowed her to weave all the different parts of the store together, as if she was conducting some sort of orchestra. Her hands fluttering across the shelves, Ginny could merchandise with her eyes closed. She didn't think, like she did when she tried to make the drinks. In weaving the food and merchandise into an appealing, stocked, and inviting store, Ginny just did the work.

Seeing her arrange everything in the store so beautifully amazed Barry. Now the mystery became "how did she do this so well"? When they sat down, Barry asked her, "Ginny, as we walked over here, what did you do?"

She was instantly alarmed by the question. Thinking she had done something wrong. "I didn't break anything, did I? Oh my gosh ... did I—?"

"No, no, no! You reset the store faster and better than anyone I've ever seen!"

Ginny smiled. "Oh, I guess so. I don't even think about that. I just know the way the store is supposed to look. I only need to look at the planograph once. Sometimes not even that. I just know."

"You're very good at it," said Barry. "Where did you learn? Who taught you?"

"Oh," she laughed. "No one taught me! I just know! It's kind of like what I was born to do."

Barry was the kind of senior manager who acted fast. In his position, he felt he had to. "Ginny, there is a regional marketing job that we're going to advertise next week. Would you like to talk to our marketing manager in Seattle? I could get her on the phone, right now."

Ginny did not hesitate. "*Yes*! Doing that would be *me*!"

Two weeks later, Ginny had found work where she could do what she did best every day.

STEWARDS IN PLACE

Taking Care

Mary Alice never knew why they picked her. Here's the story.

There were 20,000 people who had passed the standardized test to become a service rep for the state's department of unemployment. One Wednesday morning, 20 of those people sat in a waiting room on uncomfortable plastic orange chairs, waiting their turn for an interview.

Above the receptionist's desk, a TV was playing a news channel. The news segment of what happened the previous night at one of the local unemployment offices was playing for the fifth time that morning. After a two-hour wait to see a service clerk, a woman named Delores O'Banion had suddenly burst into loud, sobbing tears. By coincidence, this outburst happened at exactly the same time that a TV crew was leaving the director's office; they had just completed an interview on the latest unemployment figures.

The TV people saw an opportunity and took it. Without even introducing themselves, the glamorous young TV newswoman signaled her cameraman to start rolling, jammed a microphone in front of Delores's tear-stained face, and without even finding out why she was crying, asked, "Delores, how do you feel?"

Through her sobs, one could make out, "The President, the Governor, the unemployment office." She went on for a while, and then she said, "Because they just don't care. No one cares!"

The reporter stared earnestly into the camera, nodding at what Delores had said, then intoned, "This is Julie Sebastian reporting live from the unemployment office where Delores O'Banion has just told us that they just don't care. Back to you in the newsroom, Kevin."

At the door of the unemployment office waiting room, the associate director Frank Schultz, who had just come in to retrieve the next applicant, scanned the full room just as the reporter had said, "They just don't care."

Of the twenty people in the room, 19 ignored the TV.

Only Mary Alice, folding her arms in front of her and talking back at the TV as if it could answer, said out loud, "Yes, we do care."

Frank pointed at Mary Alice and said, "Ma'am, I believe you're next. Please come with me."

The interview went well. But Frank knew that he would hire Mary Alice within the first 10 seconds. She was a "fit" for the job. She cared. All the people in the room saw the same segment on TV. But only Mary Alice *showed* that she cared about something larger than herself—the plight of the unemployed.

Because of the stewardship for the unemployed she showed for just that one second, Frank saw something different in Mary Alice. Every applicant was qualified, passed the test, had a nice interview, and held a resume with no spelling mistakes. But Mary Alice cared, and that's what put her back to work.

Talking in Circles

Jim, Adam, and Mitch are three members of a community of 25 leaders that calls itself "Cornerstone." We met the "Cornerstone" group earlier in the book as one of its members, Chad, prepared for military deployment.

The Cornerstone Program ended many years ago, yet members of the group still feel that pull to stay in touch. That pull takes shape in big events, like military deployments. But also in the milestone events of a life, like recognizing birthdays.

The force that keeps that pull strong is an underlying "circle of stewardship." A common idea that together we are more powerful than we ever could be alone.

But the circle is not just about ideas. It also has a practical side—one's circle of stewardship can be the place where a member can go for help solving practical problems. *Like work search.*

Jim's company was expanding from the Midwest. They needed a western regional manager. Jim didn't want to wade through the detritus of job boards. He wanted someone good. Like Adam, in Denver.

When Adam took Jim's call and heard the offer, it was tempting. They were both Cornerstone. They didn't have to talk a lot. The understanding that Adam would succeed had been set down in concrete years ago. But Adam decided he was going to keep going with his own company. There was a chance that a couple of very good deals would come through very soon. If they did …

So Adam passed on the offer, but he had a thought. Adam had heard from Jodi that Mitch might be interested in doing something new. Mitch was out of the country for a week, so Jim called Lorna in Phoenix because she always had a pretty good bead on what everyone was doing in the west. Lorna told Jim to wait for Mitch. Then he called Melissa, just because he felt like running the idea past her. She was always good to talk to.

The next week Jim and Mitch met for the "job interview," which took place in a bar in Concourse A at O'Hare Airport.

A month later, Mitch was the new regional director of Jim's company. The sales meeting that year was in Tortola in the Virgin Islands.

Jim and Mitch already had their tickets.

When there is a "circle of stewardship" things get done both quicker and better.

EPILOGUE:
YOUR PERFECT JOB

This book was born during a time of record levels of unemployment across the globe. Perhaps that hardship will have lessened by the time you read these words. Perhaps not. But what will remain constant is that one does not find work by turning off their minds and sitting passively while being told what to think. You find work by doing your own thinking, following your own unique path. That gentle push down your own path begins with the Five Principles. They are the foundation. Ready for you to shape into your own path. The stories that have been included here are the prompts for you to return to again and again in developing your own new paths, your own thinking, for doing what works to connect you with work.

We've set many of these stories and played out our principles in a time when a reasonable goal for most is to connect with any type of work.

But that's not the only goal. There will always be dream jobs: world-class athlete, movie star, and famous author. Or maybe it's a need you've found that's been prompted by a story you found here. Maybe there is a way of practicing stewardship that no one's ever done before, and you're the pitch-perfect person to do it.

In your garden-variety self-help book, you'd of course be handed the steps to get there. Chock-full of clichés, it would tell you what to think, what attitude to have, maybe even what to wear to that interview that you believe in your secret deepest heart will never happen. Because much as you've tried finding a listing for "Worldwide Movie Legend" on an Internet job board, you've had no luck.

As you'd by now expect, we see it differently.

We see the Five Principles very much entwined in this final story of one person getting what he'd call his perfect job.

It's a fictional story. But it's got it all. It's got a person telling a compelling story. It's got music. The narrator communitizes like crazy. He solves all sorts of mysteries. At the end he has found work practicing stewardship in the same way this entire book has practiced stewardship: *by using the power of story to do something useful.*

So for this one last story, join us at The White House. Watch how the narrator gets his perfect job.

This is a fictional story. It never happened.

At least not yet.

My Perfect Job

"And you are? … " asked the first of what looked like many receptionists standing guard at the outer reaches of the Oval Office of President Barack Obama.

It was raining hard in Washington, D.C. I didn't have a power- broker raincoat, so my only good suit was soaked in all the worst possible places.

I needed a drink of water really badly.

"I'm ah, um … my Internet name is Chicago Guy."

"Half the people here are Chicago guys," said the receptionist over the top of her horn-rimmed glasses. "Unless of course they're Chicago gals. What we need to do is for you tell me your name, please."

I answered—too scared to speak in anything but my most earnest tones.

"Ah. I see. Well, perhaps we should call the Chief of Staff. The President is extremely busy today. If you'll have a seat, I'll … oh, here he is now. Sir, this gentleman says he's here for the one-hour lobbying session with the President."

The Chief of Staff stopped, swiveled, and stared. "Do I know you?"

"Well, no sir. Not really. I mean, I do live down the street from you back in Chicago. But no, you don't really—"

"Wait a minute. I remember talking to you and your wife when you walked past my house. She's a ballet dancer, right?"

"Yes sir, and—"

"Also took lessons from Joel Hall Dance Studios, same place I did?"

"Well, yes, but—"

"Yeah. Okay. So the reason for this little visit?"

"Well sir, this won't take long. See, I won this contest kind of thing. If you had one hour to lobby the President on anything, what would it be?"

"Well, I can tell you one thing, the President doesn't have an hour to listen to anybody about anything."

"Okay, I can do it in five minutes."

"Hey, you *are* from Chicago! What's your topic?"

"Writers."

"Writers? You mean like education? Or NEA grants or something?"

"No, writers. I'm here to lobby for writers."

"I'll give you five minutes. Let's go."

Before I could draw another breath I was in front of the President. Who actually smiled at me like he knew me!

"Cubs or Sox fan?" he asked me.

"Baseball fan, sir."

"Hah!" said the president. "Nice answer! Wrong answer, but nice one. Now, what do we got?"

"Mr. President, I'm here to ask you to consider reviving the Federal Writers' Project—a key piece of Roosevelt's Works Progress Administration—and an ideal strategy to support your plan to stimulate the economy."

"Well," laughed the President. "Believe me, I know most writers have it pretty tough these days. But we do have grants. Help me with the connection to economic stimulus here?"

"Well, I guess I'd start with this picture," I began. I handed him the first picture from my rain-soaked bag.

"Ah, the Grand Coulee Dam."

"Yes sir. A direct historical precedent to your plan to rebuild our infrastructure. Building it put 2,000 men to work. Put people to work just like you plan to do."

"Impressive project," said the President.

"Yes sir. As you know, it was one of the first times that employee health care became a factor in a job."

"And who got these jobs?" asked the President.

"They were mostly white males, sir. But they weren't all white males. Native Americans from the Colville Reservation were also hired, as were African Americans."

"Well, if you're here to convince me that it was a good idea—I already know that."

"No sir, I'm here because of the connection just one of those 2,000 men had with the project. Looking at what he did shows us a way to connect writers, and eventually all artists, with the infrastructure and economic recovery you're trying to build," I continued. "He was a sign painter, a songwriter from Okemah, Oklahoma. The Bonneville Power Administration hired this writer to do a month's worth of work. If my research is correct, they paid him $270.00. He wrote 26 songs. If I may include 2 examples of his lyrics?"

"I'm listening," said the President. I handed him a copy of the lyrics I had typed out from memory. A song that told a story of the Columbia River so well, you almost felt as if you were standing on the shore. The President scanned it in a millisecond.

"Woody Guthrie," said the President. "Let me have one more."

Surprised at his request, I handed him another. A song about the Grand Coulee Dam.

The President stared hard at the lyrics, and I had the feeling he was somewhere else. So I tried to bring him back.

"Sir, imagine we rebuild the infrastructure of the country. Who will tell the story? Do you really want it written down and recorded with PowerPoint?"

"I hear," the President smiled, "that PowerPoint makes you stupid. And I understand that Woody Guthrie really did connect infrastructure to art. But he was just one man. That all you got for me?"

"No, sir. There were 48 guidebooks written, one for each state that existed at the time. Books that were practical—telling how to get from one town to the next—but that also spoke to the history, the stories of the state. Here's one that was written about California. The detail is so rich it practically jumps up off the page."

"Now here's the point," I said hastily, as the Chief of Staff started tapping his watch.

"Imagine the story of our stewardship of this great country told not in spin-driven bullet points but with the richness of true storytellers. True writers who can bring music to the words, just like Guthrie did."

"Who wrote these books? Who were the writers of the Federal Writers' Project?" asked the President.

"Zora Neale Hurston. Saul Bellow. He wrote for the FWP. Nelson Algren, Richard Wright, Malcolm Cowley. Ralph Ellison began writing *Invisible Man* while he was working on the project. Studs Terkel, Rexroth, Patchen. Jim Thompson in Oklahoma. These were *not* big-name writers at the time. They were writers of immense talent who needed jobs like everyone else."

I took a breath and kept going. Now speaking very quickly.

"It was here, in the Federal Writers' Project, that Studs Terkel began what would eventually become his life's work of telling the story of our history in the voices of everyday working Americans."

"Which brings us to right now, today. When no one is writing the history of our times in the voices of ordinary Americans, no one connecting our challenges and pride through the common social themes that unite us all. No one to tell *their* stories of what unemployment, education, hunger, health, arts, culture, innovation, and growth mean in real people's lives."

"With no writers, we risk losing all the stories that made the country great. We could do it for very little sir. Easy."

"We?" said the President, skeptical.

"Yes sir. As fate would have it, I actually have experience running a national organization in the private sector. Managed a P/L, employed hundreds of folks."

"What did you do?" asked the President.

"Training and Customer Service."

"I like that," said the President. "Training and Customer Service. Kind of sums up what we do here."

"I found it all came down to stewardship, sir. Taking care of something bigger than we are."

"What about people?" asked the President. "Who will the writers be?"

"That's the easy part, sir. There are a lot of writers."

"I am expecting you to amaze me," said the President.

For the first time, the Chief of Staff spoke up. "Will this primarily be financed by partnerships with organizations? I mean, if you publish a book for a corporation on their corporate social responsibility, shouldn't they pay for it? If a food pantry or youth services project wants a book they can use for fund-raising, one that will give them a return on their investment—shouldn't they pay for it?"

"Well, yes, but start-up costs ..." I stammered.

He looked at the President. "Two million. That's enough. You put it back in donations to the NEA in five years when you've got at least three best-selling books. And we'll let you work out of some old offices we have in Chicago."

"If we had three million—"

"If you had nothing," the Chief of Staff smiled. "But we do have an office you could use in Chicago. You could start tomorrow."

"No," said the President.

"Start now."

So how about you?

Ready to start now?

Ready to find work even if there are no jobs?

ACKNOWLEDGEMENTS

Producing a book is a team sport. My hope is that all those I've spoken with about this book, and changing the way people find work, consider themselves part of the team. My sincere thanks.

Tom Dickinson's encouragement through all the years is at the foundation of everything I've ever written. The people of the premier Literary E-Zine on the web, "Fictionique," and the blog sites, "Open Salon" and "Our Salon," have given me the chance to sit at the table with writers who are my heroes.

Without Lisa Phillips and her editorial wisdom, the book in your hands would not exist. Without Dennis Welch, you wouldn't know about the book. Jean Haider, Janis Dowd and my brother Warren's insight was invaluable. David Brown, co-author of "I am Your Neighbor: Voices from a Chicago Food Pantry," always helps when I write anything.

Yvonne Parks and Pear Creative brilliantly designed the book while I watched in awe.

Every book is the result of what a writer has learned from those who came before. So a personal thanks to the world class thought leaders Bob Beaudine, Curt Coffman Anderson Schoenrock and U.S. Representative Jan Schakowsky (IL – 9th Congressional District). And a message of appreciation to: Jim Collins, Tom Rath, Daniel Levitin, and Peter Senge.

For all who see themselves in these stories, and to the leaders, artists, musicians and writers whose work flows between these lines, my deepest thanks and gratitude.

Finally, this book is for the millions of people who, like me, have had to find work when there are no jobs.

Let's keep the conversation going. Visit us at www.findingwork.org

CPSIA information can be obtained at www.ICGtesting.com
Printed in the USA
LVOW101957140513

333636LV00005B/10/P